NOT FOR WOMEN ONLY

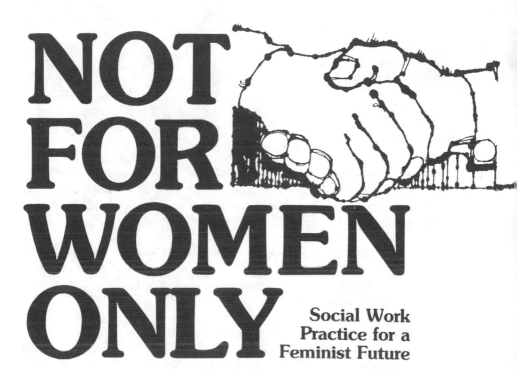

Social Work Practice for a Feminist Future

Editors

Mary Bricker-Jenkins   Nancy R. Hooyman

Based on an Institute on Feminist Practice presented by
the NASW National Committee on Women's Issues at the
NASW Professional Symposium, Washington, DC, November 1983.

National Association of Social Workers, Inc.
Silver Spring, Maryland 20910

Cover design by Johanna Vogelsang
Interior design by Gloria Gentile

© 1986 by the National Association of Social Workers, Inc.
First impression, 1989

Library of Congress Cataloging-in-Publication Data

Institute on Feminist Practice (1983: Washington, D.C.)
    Not for women only.

    "Based on an Institute on Feminist Practice presented by the NASW National Committee on Women's Issues at the NASW Professional Symposium, Washington, D.C., November 1983."
    Bibliography: p. 123.
    1. Feminism—United States—Congresses.   2. Women social workers—United States—Congresses.   I. Bricker-Jenkins, Mary.
II. Hooyman, Nancy.   III. National Committee on Women's Issues.
IV. National Association of Social Workers.   V. Title.
HQ1403.I56   1983   305.4'2'0973   85-28532
ISBN 0-87101-131-X

Printed in the United States of America

Dedication

Four years ago, having entered a doctoral program with grave doubts and cynicism about my ability to get through without compromising my soul, I made an appointment to see the man who had been assigned as my adviser. "Everyone in this school knows my radical feminist politics," I thought, as I approached his door. "They are doing this to let me know who's boss around here. They think a little 'D & B' is good for the soul!"

Bob Mayer answered the door. Over a foot and half taller than I, with a full red beard and brilliant eyes, he greeted me with a gentleness and warmth that instantly challenged my assumptions. I was shaken.

He asked me, as advisers are wont to do, what I wanted to get out of the program and what my life was to be. I responded with some fuzzy ideas about feminism and social work. He would not let it be. "But what do you want to *do*?" he insisted. "Well, Bob, I want to change the world." "That's it!" he said. "Remember that goal every day you come here. Don't change it, don't compromise it, don't forget it for a moment. Do everything you do here with that purpose in mind. If I see you doing otherwise, I will tell you what I see. I want this for you. I want this for me. I want it for all of us."

The Institute on Feminist Practice—indeed, all my work on the Feminist Practice Project—has been a step in the process of social transformation. Along with Bob, I want a world in which the full potential of each person can unfold, a world willing to risk nonviolence and diversity and gentleness. I hoped that Bob would be able to share his feminist views at the institute, but he died on November 3, 1983, shortly before the institute convened. Nevertheless, he inspired the title of the institute: "Not for Women Only: Social Work Practice for a Feminist Future."

Many of you will remember Bob Mayer as an author, an activist, a former dean, and a teacher who brought cooperative problem-solving principles to the classroom. I want you to know him also as I knew him—as a grinning, gentle giant who daily went about the work of changing the world.

MARY BRICKER-JENKINS

When Bob died, his wife, Ruth Brandwein, was with him. It was an expression of Bob's feminism that he resigned as dean of the School of Social Work at Bryn Mawr College to move to New York to be with the woman he married. Bob and Ruth shared the dream of infusing feminist principles into their work as administrators. Bob saw his role as supporting Ruth's efforts to do so at the State University of New York at Stony Brook, where she is dean. The greatest challenge to men who are changing is to give up their privileges. Bob struggled to do that.

And how much we all benefit from the work of the woman he encouraged! Ruth's work as a feminist author, educator, and activist is well known. Her warm personal style as administrator reflects her feminist values. As a single parent for most of her career, she has been empathic toward and supportive of other women who are struggling to integrate their personal and professional lives. Chairperson of the Council on Social Work Education's Women's Commission from 1980 to 1983, she confronted patriarchy in social work education and insisted on speaking about differences. "We are not a 'special' population!" she said recently. "In social work, we *are* the population." Ruth has presented these truths and differences in a way that calls forth courage and compels action.

We wish to dedicate this work to Bob and to Ruth. We ask that you join us in drawing strength and confidence from Bob's life as we shape our visions and in sending Ruth the healing energies we create through our work together.

Nancy R. Hooyman

Preface

The National Association of Social Workers (NASW) established the National Committee on Women's Issues (NCOWI) in 1975. The major goals of NCOWI have been to work for the ratification of the Equal Rights Amendment, improve social work practice with women, monitor NASW's affirmative action plan, encourage and assist chapters to form women's issues committees, and move women up in the profession. Toward these ends, NCOWI held its first NASW Conference on Social Work Practice with Women in 1980, entitled "Social Work Practice in Sexist Society."[1] The conference was a great success, and the second national conference on women is planned for 1986.

NCOWI has been involved in various major projects for the enhancement of women in social work. One such project is the Feminist Practice Project, funded by a special grant from NASW's Program Advancement Fund. The aims of the project are to identify, analyze, and describe politically oriented models of social work practice with and for women that are based on feminist theory. Another project was the Institute on Feminist Practice, held at the NASW Professional Symposium, November 1983, in Washington, D.C. This book is based on papers presented at the institute. The recurring theme of the articles is the identification of feminist practice and perspectives in different arenas of social work endeavors. As the authors state, although these papers emerged from women's experiences with oppression, consciousness raising, and reconstructive action, the models of feminist practice presented herein are "not for women only."

Both of the aforementioned projects were inspired by Mary Bricker-Jenkins and Nancy R. Hooyman—dynamic leaders in the feminist movement. As a Chicana, feminist, and chairperson of NCOWI, I want to express my appreciation to these two outstanding feminists who have fostered our understanding by bringing women's issues to the forefront of the profession.

NCOWI expresses its appreciation to the participants of the Institute on Feminist Practice who shared with us their problems, joys, and challenges of being feminists. We value the love, support, and constant stimulation given us by our sisters.

MARTHA MOLINA FIMBRES, *Chairperson*
National Committee on Women's Issues
June 1985   *National Association of Social Workers*

---

[1]See Ann Weick and Susan T. Vandiver, eds., *Women, Power, and Change,* selected papers from Social Work Practice in Sexist Society, First NASW Conference on Social Work Practice with Women (Washington, D.C.: National Association of Social Workers, 1981).

Contents

Lesbians

Men and Feminist Practice

Spirituality and Healing

BE NOBODY'S DARLING

Be nobody's darling;
Be an outcast.
Take the contradictions
Of your life
And wrap around
you like a shawl,
To parry stones
To keep you warm.

Alice Walker

Introduction

This book developed from the commitment of NASW's National Committee on Women's Issues (NCOWI) to the advancement of feminist practice. NCOWI's commitment, in turn, evolved from the first National Conference on Social Work Practice in Sexist Society held in September 1980. Over 800 women from around the country gathered at that conference. In both the large formal sessions and spontaneous small groups, women shared their common visions, as well as their sense of being alone in their efforts to empower women in their communities.

At that conference and at subsequent gatherings, several themes emerged repeatedly: empowerment, human liberation, meeting human needs, the individual's dignity within the context of collective responsibility, the transformation of personal and social relations, and healing. Woven into the fabric of feminist practice, these themes are not new, but rather basic to social work's history and traditions, especially to the tradition that frames all professional activity with considerations of social justice and human liberation. Nevertheless, the theory, values, and assumptions that dominate the profession today often differ from those that are basic to feminist practice.

To reclaim our feminist tradition in social work and to articulate clearly feminist principles in light of the current realities of practice, NCOWI developed the Feminist Practice Project. The Feminist Practice Project is a national research study that aims to describe and disseminate information on feminist practice and to evolve new models of practice grounded in feminist theory and values. It recognizes that the concept "the personal is political" is core to our practice but that the concept will vary with the historical and material conditions to which practitioners respond. NCOWI has, therefore, assumed that feminist practice models are diverse and must be shared widely to advance our practice.

The 1983 Presymposium Institute, "Not for Women Only: Practice for a Feminist Future," evolved from a pilot study of the project. It represented a collective effort to share the ways in which practitioners advance their feminist agenda in their daily work. The presenters at the institute offered several different perspectives on feminist practice that illustrate some of the many ways in which feminism, political orientation, and life experience are blended to form distinct approaches to analysis and work. They detailed the theory, values, assumptions, and purposes that inform their practice. As each presenter spoke and others recognized aspects of their own practice, excitement and energy were generated. Women who had previous felt alone in their struggles were affirmed by hearing their beliefs and feelings echoed by others. Contradictions, fears, doubts, hopes, prejudices, and misconceptions were shared, at first tentatively and then more openly as both female and male participants listened and trusted. When the institute came to a close, there was also sadness—sadness that our time together was limited and that the institute would reach only a small number of women and men. We agreed on the importance of trying to capture some of the day's richness and diversity through a publication. Thus, this book was born.

The book includes each of the presentations, as well as selections from feminist poetry, music, and other forms of cultural work. These selections were included because we learned in the pilot study of the major influence that women's culture has had on the work of feminist practitioners. Perhaps these art forms capture the reality of women's lives far better than can the traditional social work literature. And, to paraphrase political organizer and musician Barbara Dane, we must take back control of our own culture. To do that, we need to understand the nature of culture. We have been taught to think of culture as something esoteric and "above" us or as something frivolous and not meaningful. Neither conception is correct, and both can be harmful. For culture is the symbolic basis for human communication, expressing and supporting the connections among us. When we give over control of culture to those who would control and exploit us, they will use that power to make us feel separate, ignorant, and weak. When we take it back, we take back our history, we engage in struggle, we create our future.[1]

This book portrays a practice rooted in a rich tradition of social action and struggle, selectively incorporating professional theory and methods and open to the influences of both traditional and nontraditional helpers and healers. Although they emerge from women's experiences with oppression, consciousness raising, and reconstructive action, the models of feminist practice presented in here are clearly not for women only.

MARY BRICKER-JENKINS AND NANCY R. HOOYMAN

---

[1]Barbara Dane, line notes from *I Hate the Capitalist System* (Brooklyn, N.Y.: Paredon Records, 1973), pp. 9–10.

URGED TO DENY THE SECRETS

Urged to deny the secrets within our natures
And to reject the differences of others,
We are taught to be fearful of ourselves
and contemptuous of others.
Separated from ourselves and isolated from each other,
We are taught to huddle together for comfort
Under the socially acceptable banners
Of racism, sexism, classism, and homophobia—
We are discouraged from seeing the ways in which
We are all connected.
We are thus rendered powerless
And immobilized by our prejudices.
This is not an accident.

BLANCHE WIESEN COOK

From "Female Support Networks and Political Activism: Lilian Wald, Crystal Eastman, Emma Goldman, Jane Addams" by Blanche Wiesen Cook. Copyright © 1977 by Blanche Wiesen Cook. First appeared in *Chrysalis* (Autumn 1977); reprinted in *Women and Support Networks* (Brooklyn, N.Y.: Out and Out Books, 1979). Reprinted by permission of the author.

A Feminist World View: Ideological Themes from the Feminist Movement

Mary Bricker-Jenkins
Nancy R. Hooyman

Those who practice and teach from a feminist perspective often meet skepticism and critical questioning from colleagues, which, in effect, convey, "What do women want now?" What is feminist social work practice? What are its predominant structural characteristics, its value orientations, and its techniques? What are its aims? Does it have a theory base that can be articulated? How does it differ from advocacy and other politically oriented social work practice or from "good" social work practice?

What distinguishes feminist practice is the centrality of its ideology. Although all practice embodies ideologies, few practitioners make their ideologies explicit and consciously examine their performance against their ideologies. For feminist practitioners, ideology is the core of practice—the measure of all choices to be made—and is consciously used to motivate and evaluate action. In addition, feminist practitioners purposefully seek and

Mary Bricker-Jenkins, MSW, is a movement activist and organizer whose interest in feminist practice and the common cause of workers and clients is rooted in her involvement in the welfare rights movement. With a practice background in public welfare, child and family services, and community development, she has taught social welfare history and policy and generalist practice at several colleges and universities. She now lives and works in the hills of Tennessee, where she continues her research as coordinator of the Feminist Practice Project and has an active public practice.

Nancy R. Hooyman, MSW, Ph.D., associate dean of the School of Social Work, University of Washington, Seattle, and a co-consultant to the Feminist Practice Project, has a practice background in community organization, particularly with low-income women. As an activist with older women, her work involves bringing a feminist perspective to research on caregiving and the elderly and identifying the common ground among women of all ages. She also is working to identify and create the administrative and organizational conditions that support feminist practice.

highly value the congruence of practice goals, process, structure, and program with feminist ideology.

Ideology, as it is used in this article, contains elements of theory as well as beliefs and values. As Gould defined it:

> Ideology is a pattern of beliefs and concepts (both factual and normative) which purport to explain complex social phenomena with a view to directing and simplifying socio-political choices facing individuals and groups.[1]

Ginsberg distinguished "open" and "closed" ideologies, the latter being "self-contained systems demanding all or none commitment."[2] Feminist ideology is an open system in the Ginsberg model; criticized from within and open to exchange with other ideologies, it advances through dialogue.

As a countervailing ideology (and as a social movement), feminism insists on a critical examination of the individual and collective choices that shape women's lives. Those choices, in turn, are measured against the imperatives of human need and social justice; feminism insists on removing any sanction from choices that are judged to be inimical to human development, freedom, and health. Feminists may argue the details of analysis and program, but an underlying consensus exists: that barriers to the realization of the full and unique human potential of women can and must be challenged and changed.[3] Moreover, those barriers are identified and alternatives fashioned through consciousness-raising and collective action; we women claim the right to name the world according to our experience of it, and we take responsibility for changing what does not fit our experience.

Feminist ideology is organic. As an outgrowth of consciousness raising and collective action, it is subject to constant scrutiny. When it has not been constantly scrutinized, it has turned on itself and violated its first principle. Feminist ideology is grounded in women's experience of the world but that world is constantly changing by the actions of women. This is the nature of "praxis," which is at the core of feminist theory and practice: "Theory follows from practice and is impossible to develop in the absence of practice, because our theory is that practising our practice is our theory."[4] Feminist theory and values are, by definition, ever tentative, never absolute, and always becoming.

Nevertheless, some enduring themes in feminist literature can be identified that are interrelated and thereby constitute an ideology. In Table 1 (see page 6), major ideological themes and their subthemes are presented. These themes are an end to patriarchy, empowerment, process, the personal is political, unity-diversity, validation of the nonrational, and consciousness raising/praxis. No attempt has been made to resolve the many important theoretical debates among feminists of various "tendencies" (radical, socialist, or liberal/reformist) in the movement; thus, the presentation of ideological themes is neither exhaustive nor without internal contradictions. Nor would all feminists agree on all the elements presented. Feminist ideology allows for the existence of those contradictions; the ideology—and the social movement—are built on contradictions.

END TO PATRIARCHY

Patriarchy, as the institutionalized system of male domination and privilege, is the mechanism that ensures women's subordination. Similar to all such systems, patriarchy carries an authoritative set of assumptions, beliefs, and theories to support it. Having been so long in ascendancy, patriarchal ideology has also determined the interpretation and recording of history. Therefore, we women must reclaim history, exposing the myths that distort our experiences and limit our vision of our capabilities. Patriarchy has protected itself by guarding knowledge and controlling its distribution, thereby conveying that major systems of knowledge and skills were too complex and inaccessible to average people (many men and most women). Thus, the task of feminists is to demystify and make available the knowledge and skills that people must have to solve problems and meet their needs.

Under the patriarchal allocation of rights, privilege, and responsibilities, women have been assigned the preservation of certain values; our historical experience has reinforced these values and shaped others. Such "feminine" values include respect for and the preservation of human life, concern for the individual's dignity and worth, and the nurturance of social structures that promote human development. For many feminists, these values have led to a commitment to nonviolence, which, as Demming noted, "incorporates traditionally 'feminine' values by actively promoting a continuing concern for individual welfare, social healing, and respect for life."[5]

According to Kaplan, a "female consciousness" is shared by all women, whether feminist or not; this consciousness is rooted in the expectation that women take primary responsibility for the protection and nurturance of human life and the meeting of basic human needs.[6] This consciousness has thus been the source of seemingly spontaneous and "irrational" collective actions by women that are women's attempts to perform responsibilities by infusing our values into political discourse and historical orientations:

> By placing human need above other social and political requirements and human life above property, profit, and even individual rights, female consciousness creates the vision of a society that has not yet appeared.[7]

Feminist theory does not prescribe the specific features of an alternative social order; indeed, to do so would contradict that theory. However, certain value-based chracteristics that are rooted in women's experiences are considered essential. As Berlin noted, "the human values that women were previously assigned to preserve [become] central organizing principles for a new social order."[8] As the struggle continues to advance those organizing principles— as women take concrete action to effect social healing and the affirmation of human values—the system's inability to respond to such demands by relying on domination and exploitation of people and natural resources becomes

Table 1. Feminist Ideological Themes

End to Patriarchy

Demystify and demythicize; reclaim history

Meet human needs; respect life

Transform personal and social relationships; end all systems of
subordination and privilege

Value women's perspectives and experiences

Empowerment

"Power" reconceptualized as limitless, collective, and transactive

Implies individual responsibility, not individual property

Egalitarianism; no "power over"

Enabling, nonviolent problem solving

Inclusiveness; making common cause

Process

Process as product; ends in the means

Must be prefigurative, culture building, nonoppressive

Must educate, democratize, enable leadership and responsibility

"We're all in process"; nonjudgmental

Nonlinear, dynamic; consciousness and conditions are ever changing

Developmental; effectiveness, as well as efficiency

The Personal Is Political

Personal problems and conditions have historical, material, and
cultural bases and dimensions

We are all connected; there are no personal private solutions

Failure to act is to act

Achieve personal growth through political action, "taking charge"

Change selves, change the world

Orientation to fundamental structural change

Unity-Diversity

None is free until all are free

Sisterhood, solidarity

Respect differences, preserve uniqueness; diversity as a source of
strength and growth

Conflict is inevitable; peace is achievable

Elimination of false dichotomies and artificial separations

Synthesis and wholeness

Table 1. Continued

Validation of the Nonrational

Healing
Spirituality
Nonlinear, multidimensional thinking
Reintegrating public and private spheres
Process of defining problems is recognized as subjective
Multiple competing definitions of problems; many "truths"

Consciousness raising / Praxis

Renaming = recreating reality
Liberation through one's own actions; self-reliance
"Rugged collectivism"
Influsion of consciousness and values in material world
Revolution as process, not event

increasingly clear. Underscoring the radical potential of liberal feminist action, Eisenstein indicated that even innocuous "reformist" demands—for equal pay, adequate child care, the protection of civil rights, and so on—confound the very social order that gave them legitimacy:

> Mainstream feminist demands derive from the promises of liberalism as an ideology—individual autonomy and independence, freedom of choice, equality of opportunity, and equality before the law...[But] feminist demands uncover the truth that capitalist patriarchal society cannot deliver on its "liberal" promises of equality or even equal rights for women without destabilizing itself.[9]

Therefore, attempts to create personal and social relations that enable the protection and preservation of the values women are expected to guard lead inexorably to the recognition of a need for a fundamentally transformed, nonexploitive social order, however, dim its features may appear or however unachievable it may seem.[10] The features of this social order are discovered through the respectful exploration of our no longer devalued experiences.

EMPOWERMENT

Feminism reconceptualizes power. This recasting of the concept and the power yields another fundamental organizing principle of feminist practice. In the patriarchal lexicon, power is a "market" concept; it is presumed to be a finite resource that, if one is to have and wield it, must be appropriated and managed.

One's power, as a commodity that can be individually "owned," is rooted in one's ability to dominate and control others. By contrast, feminists return to the concept its original meaning, "to be able"—from the Latin, *posse*. In this sense, power is derived from the ability to realize potential and to accomplish aspirations and values. Power is rooted in energy, strength, and effective communication, and it is limitless.[11] Indeed, power expands, becoming increasingly collective and inclusive as more people are able to grow to their fullest potential. To have "power over," as practiced in hierarchical and individualistic systems, actually precludes empowerment in the sense of enabling.

Thus, the feminist conceptualization of power is of a force and energy that is inherently noncoercive and which is oriented to liberating the strength and energy of women and others. Feminist concepts of power occur within the context of a world view in which all are connected and therefore each is responsible for the well-being of the whole. Empowerment takes place as feminist values are observed in the process of seeking a common ground and making common cause with each other. As Thorne stated:

> In working for political change, feminists seek to create organizations based on power understood as energy and initiative, while challenging institutions that embody power understood as domination. Although fraught with contradictions, the feminist process uses methods of organization as a strategy for redefining political power itself.[12]

The view that power is limitless leads to a setting aside of competitiveness, which is based on win-lose, zero-sum thinking.

This conceptualization does not mean, however, that feminist practitioners deny the historically and materially rooted power and status differentials that have kept women (and many men) "in their place," excluding them from the arenas in which control over material resources is decided and the development of culture is charted. However, it does recognize the transactive nature of power, in other words, that we women participate in the construction and maintenance of personal and social relations if only by our silent acquiescence. Therefore, we can and must withdraw our sanction from those relations and processes that are incompatible with our interests and values: human liberation and empowerment. To do otherwise is to give over our power to others, who cannot be expected to guard our interests.

PROCESS

Inherent in the feminist system of belief is the notion that process is of utmost importance, particularly at those critical moments when we are most tempted to abandon it in the interest of "efficiency." Unlike most revolutionary movements, feminism insists on preserving the ends in the means and on the compatibility of method and vision.[13] Because our actions on the world constantly are changing the world (and us), the world will evolve along the lines we want it to only as we create it moment by moment through "prefigurative" actions—those that reflect feminist values and therefore advance these values historically and materially. To violate our vision in our process is to sabotage it, for we cannot advance theory/practice without a historical and material base. Again, "our theory is that practising our practice is our theory."[14]

Attention to process, when coupled with direct action through the delivery of needed services, is intended to fulfill two functions in the politics of transformation:

> We may identify not only a *politics of struggle*, but also a *politics of function* (Dennison, 1972). The former is what is usually meant by politics— the direct confrontation and struggle against the powers that be. But, by the latter, we mean that an organization is political if, in its very form, it exemplifies the sort of democratically run, community-based organization that could provide a model for a new society. Insofar as worker-managed organizations fulfill vital social needs (for food, housing, health care, education, etc.) in a democratic manner, they are engaged in a politics of function.[15]

Thus, process is seen as an important product in and of itself, and its production through nonoppressive means builds culture—an integrated material and symbolic system around an alternative value set—thereby demonstrating the viability of the value set and ensuring its survival. Knowing that the structure and process of education convey messages that we are as powerful as the content of education, feminist practitioners seek to educate through example and provide opportunities for people to develop requisite knowledge, skills, and attitudes to support responsible democratic action. The value placed on process means that feminist practitioners include "correct process" as a criterion for judging performance.

As a corollary, however, there is an understanding that "we are all in process" and that the dynamic, nonlinear process will not be smooth. The dominant culture's attitudes, values, and skills are carried into our relationships and structures; therefore, we feminists must be tolerant of ourselves and each other as we display less-than-perfect politics. Moreover, "being in process" means that we are constantly changing our conditions and our consciousness. Our visions and our methods for achieving them must be rooted in current historical conditions as well as in our expanding world view. Our doctrine is that we cannot be doctrinaire.

THE PERSONAL IS POLITICAL

The notion that the personal is political is a primary analytic tool in feminist practice—a precision instrument with which we examine the myths and structures of oppression that contain us. It also is another of the fundamental organizing principles of our practice: we change our world by changing our selves as we change our world. It is by this process that fundamental structural changes may occur.

Our feelings about ourselves and our conditions—our consciousness—are shaped by political forces. These forces have been controlled primarily by others. To change that situation, we must impose ourselves on historical processes and material conditions and, in so doing, expose as false the myths of our powerlessness and dependence. This imposition, however, must take cognizance of our interconnectedness; just as no "private realities" exist apart from political processes, there are no private solutions. Given that we are interconnected and that the sum of our individual actions create the social order, we are thereby responsible to each other for our actions. Accordingly, failure to act is to act; likewise, failure to work to transform social and political realities is to support the status quo. Therefore, the only reasonable course of action is to "take charge" by engaging in political action. We feminists shape our individual destinies through collective action precisely because no individual can "take charge" without the occurrence of collective action. The personal is political.

What this means for the daily reality of feminist practitioners is that energy and resources will be directed to those material conditions that women experience as most oppressive and debilitating—poor housing, numbing work, inept health care, nonnutritious food, inadequate child care, danger on the streets—and against the victim-blaming ideologies that prevent effective action to change these conditions.[16] Accordingly, the constituency of feminist practitioners (clients, students, and colleagues) must be fully active in all phases of the problem-solving process. Reciprocity—the sharing of experiences and perspectives, skills, and energy—marks the "therapeutic" exchange in which the practitioner and the client make common cause on issues of shared concerns.[17] Moreover, there are no experts in the process whose roles are confined to stimulating or observing changes.

In the process of taking collective action to change the historical, material, and cultural conditions reflected in clients' shattered images and personalized in their psychic pains, we expect to change our *selves* as much as anything else. As Piercy said: "If what we seek to change does not change us, we are playing with blocks."[18] Risk taking assumes a new dimension to feminist practitioners.

UNITY-DIVERSITY

Solidarity has been an anchoring theme in all revolutionary movements, for obvious pragmatic reasons. Feminism develops a new variation on this theme with its affirmation of diversity as a source of strength and as a potentially powerful organizing tool in building the movement. Out of struggles to understand and eliminate all forms of oppression from the feminist movement, feminists have struggled to deal with racism, classism, heterosexism, ableism, anti-Semitism, and the like. Indeed, any form of institutionalized behavior that advances the interests of some at the expense of others or prevents the actualization of innate human potential is subject to scrutiny and corrective action.[19]

These struggles lead first to a tolerance of diversity and then, on deeper analysis and action, to a valuing of it. Consistent with the collectivist ethic of feminism is the view that building sisterhood involves making available to each the unique experiences of all. This process expands our consciousness and our capacity for growth and adaptation. As in nature, those most able to adapt and survive in hostile environments are those with genetic diversity. Similarly, in problem solving and the creation of new social relations, we are strengthened by the richness of diverse solutions to the problems of living in patriarchal cultures and attempting to transform them.

Just as power is not a zero-sum commodity, personal growth in consciousness and ability is not a finite entity for which to compete. When we understand that our sister's success at being who she is does not diminish us, then we can support her growth even if her way is not our way. Indeed, solidarity is developed when we explore together the fact that others benefit from our separateness and fear of each other. When we discover who benefits, we realize that it is no accident that we have been taught that we cannot all work together. Then we begin to understand that, given our connectedness and the virulence of systems of oppression and alienation, each individual's freedom is secure only when her sisters also are free.

Although this line of reasoning has been advanced before, our diversity has seldom been used as a basis for a movement. We have been taught to build organizations on the basis of similarities. Building on diversity is fraught with contradictions and therefore difficult to practice. Nevertheless, sisterhood is built on such contradictions, which we seek to resolve in a manner that preserves uniqueness, protects each individual and group from exploitation, and maximizes freedom and self-actualization. Inevitably, this work involves conflict. However, conflict does not preclude peace. Rather, if managed in noncoercive ways it can lead to peace by creating the conditions for it.

Therefore, feminist practitioners will not only strive to eliminate racism, classism, heterosexism, anti-Semitism, ableism, and other systems of oppression and exploitation, but will affirm the need for diversity by actively reaching out to achieve it. The elimination of status differentials, of expert-nonexpert dichotomies, is an effort to remove all forms of domination-subordination from our practice. The use of noncompetitive working principles and noncoercive conflict resolution are attempts to promote the presence of diversity in our practice. Out of such diversity, synthesis can be achieved, rather than separateness and false dichotomies. Although it is not yet well developed as a practice strategy, this approach of advancing diversity, when refined, will undoubtedly move our theory-practice substantially forward. It will expand our organizing base to include those we have unwittingly excluded by imposing categories and status labels that obscure our common interests.

VALIDATION OF THE NONRATIONAL

By controlling the process of who asks the questions and who defines the problems, patriarchal systems have attempted to objectify social problems in "facts." The translation of facts into social problems, however, is not an objective, "rational," scientific process, as we have been led to believe. Instead, the process of defining problems is always subjective, shaped by values, interests, and ideologies. Every problem has multiple competing definitions, none of which necessarily are right or wrong. The truth we seek does not exist. Instead, there are many truths, and their discovery begins in a subjective "naming" process— not with the learning of someone else's language, categories, and analyses.

In contrast to the rationality, linear thinking, and analytical processes that are valued by contemporary patriarchal cultures, spirituality, multidimensional thinking, and synthesis are treasured by feminists.[20] Personal and social healing, both enduring themes in our work, are based on the ancient arts and rituals practiced by women as well as on the knowledge and skills we have developed in the service professions. Contrary to the conceptual and material dichotomies and polarities of patriarchy, part of the healing process in which we are engaged involves reintegrating and restoring the bifurcated dimensions of our lives, such as the split of life work into public and private spheres, to "wholeness."[21]

As a result, a feminist practice setting often resembles a "cottage industry." When "domestic" activities are undertaken at the work or meeting place, all workers are involved in their performance. This collective action underscores the concepts of individual responsibility for the total life of the community and of sisterhood and solidarity. Time and energy for attention to workers' personal needs and feelings are protected. Emotionality, as a part of the personal experience that is the basis for all authentic knowledge and action, is reintroduced into all aspects of work life.

The involvement of the "whole person," which is expected in feminist practice, creates an intense experience, particularly because most people have been trained since childhood to avoid mixing business with pleasure and to leave their feelings at the office door (or plant gate). Open interpersonal conflict may be intensified in feminist practice settings; it is this openness—not the existence of conflict per se—that distinguishes feminist practice settings from other work environments. Time and energy also are given to nurturing and healing; in some settings, spiritual rituals and ceremonies may be part of the work process.[22]

In short, the feminist approach does not diminish rationality, order, and efficiency, but, rather, restores to the "public" sphere dimensions of human experience and capability that have long been excluded.

CONSCIOUSNESS RAISING AND PRAXIS

The work of feminists involves consciousness raising that is explicitly directed to social transformation:

> Central to feminist theory and feminist method...is consciousness-raising. Through this process, feminists confront the reality of women's condition by examining their experience and by taking this analysis as the starting

point for individual and social change. By its nature, this method of inquiry challenges traditional notions of authority and objectivity and opens a dialectical questioning of existing power structures, or our own experience, and of theory itself.[23]

Consciousness raising is thus seditious in its intent and, if we stay with it, in its ultimate effect. Its outcome is a new set of values, assumptions, and expectations, embodied in a new set of structures and personal and social relationships.

Since consciousness raising is at the core of feminist theory and method, it is an essential part of an evolving, often implicit, theory of social change that underpins feminist practice.[24] This underlying theory of social change appears to contain the following assumptions and propositions:[25]

■ Social transformation involves the infusion of feminist (or, perhaps, feminine) consciousness and values into historical processes and the material and symbolic worlds: "Women's qualities must become public values."[26]

■ Essential to this process is consciousness raising: "the process by which men [and women], not as recipients, but as knowing subjects, achieve a deepening awareness both of the sociocultural reality which shapes their lives and of their capacity to transform that reality through action upon it."[27]

■ Consciousness raising is a healing process that begins with renaming reality according to our own experience. Renaming reality involves rejecting names (words, language, symbols) that are not grounded directly in our experience but which, because we have adopted them, have the effect of containing and controlling us. As MacLeod and Bedard put it, "Our self-hatred ends where our analysis begins."[28]

■ The aim of consciousness raising is praxis—the theory-practice dialectic through which we collectively understand and shape reality: As Lindemann explained, "Words are grounded in past action(s) and consideration of these words leads to proposed new actions. New actions lead to further reflection. . . ."[29]

■ "Reality" is a political as well as a social construction: "We make history, or it makes us."[30] Therefore, we are each personally responsible for our contribution to the shaping of reality and thus personally responsible to each other. As a corollary, we are liberated only through our own actions—our participation in an unfolding collective process.

■ Interpersonal and social relationships are part of the same network of relationships that constitute the structural framework of our lives; we cannot change one without the other, any more than we can change our selves without changing our relationships (and vice-versa).[31] A corollary is this: If we reflect the same values in our interpersonal and our social relationships and structures, we reinforce those values and enable their concrete expression. Our vision of a new social order incorporates a vision of the transformation and the liberation of our most intimate lives.

■ The small group, particularly the self-help group, is a basic unit of political action for social transformation. By providing in microcosm the experience of personal-political transformation, the small group advances it in the larger world. Gordon and Hunter expanded on this theme, as follows:

> The model of collective self-help...strengthens the connection between personal and social change. In the best of cases, self-help groups *combine consciousness raising with material aid* and an opening to a new community of people; thus *providing not only the ideas but some of the conditions for adopting a less passive stance towards the world.* The self-help model is a way of dealing with the fact that politics often becomes a part of one's life only when a political problem is directly experienced.[32] [Italics added.]

■ Because our consciousness and values are not in ascendancy, it is imperative that we build an alternative culture with alternative institutions and symbolic representations (language, art, environments, and so forth) that reflect on consciousness and values. There are two reasons that such a culture is essential: (1) an alternative culture is "protective," enabling the kind of reinforcement of a world view that is necessary for its transmission and institutionalization[33] and (2) it provides a concrete arena for the testing of our theory and practice—a historical and material grounding for our work that preserves its integrity and enables it to advance.

■ As Cook observed, "revolution is a process, not an event."[34] We cannot wait until "after the revolution" to make things right. Rather, we must assume responsibility for our decisions and actions, examine the political implications of our choices, and see the ends in the means.

■ Although the development of alternative institutions and symbols is essential, it is not sufficient. The development of a "critical mass"—the accumulation of contradictions to the point of paradigmatic crisis and change—will not happen by "cultural accretion," but by sustained political struggle, as reflected in the conclusions drawn by Rothschild-Whitt and Lindenfeld:

> As this history of social change in America reveals, alternative institutions have played a crucial role in transforming our society, beginning with the pivotal contribution they made to the American Revolution. Without a broader political movement with which to align themselves, however, they have been insufficient as agents of social change.[35]

The implications of this underlying theory of social change for feminist practice, in addition to those already indicated, include the following:

■ There will be a minimal use of "rules," except those agreed to by consensus and constantly subject to scrutiny. Authority does not derive from status, tradition, or credentials because part of the process of consciousness raising is to "question authority." The only authority that is legitimated is the authority conferred by the collectivity, whether by practitioners to practitioners or by constituents to practitioners.

■ Self-help groups will be emphasized among practitioners and among constituents, although the struggle for adequate services from the state will not cease.

■ In addition to the conscious creation of alternative institutions, practitioners will engage in culture building by attending to symbolic representations: language, the physical layout of the office, and the use of art, literature, and music. However, such cultural work must be connected to political struggle. Thus, feminists emphasize coalition building, rank-and-file union activity, support for interest groups, and caucuses established for survival and self-advocacy from a sense of shared concerns.

■ Research, which can be viewed as a form of consciousness raising, has similar characteristics: it is ongoing, often phenomenological, and action oriented. It shares an epistemology with the concept of praxis and is a form of praxis, as Freire noted:

> ...it is necessary to start an investigation with a preoccupation in trying to understand the dialectical relationship between objectivity and subjectivity. If I perceive reality as the dialectical relationship between objectivity and subjectivity, then I have to use methods for investigation which involve the people of the area being studied as researchers. They should take part in the investigations themselves and not serve as passive objects of the study...Thus, in doing research, I am educating and being educated with the people...to the extent that we put into practice the plans resulting from the investigations, we change the levels of consciousness of the people, and by this change, research again. Thus, there is a dynamic movement between researching and acting on the results of the research.[36]

Research by feminist practitioners is essential; and it is a revolutionary act.

Although we cannot succumb to naivete about the nature of the struggle or the fact that it is a protracted one which requires a long view of history, there are many indications in our environment (such as the sanctuary movement, anti-apartheid struggles, the growth of nonviolent peace activism in Europe and North America, and the reclamation of traditional spiritual, social, and political practices) that people are searching for an alternative that is healing, gentle, egalitarian, and empowering.[37] We have a long and enduring history of struggle to implement such values as egalitarianism, consensus democracy, nonexploitation, cooperation, collectivism, diversity, and nonjudgmental spirituality even though these values are not ascendant in the American tradition. In the fabric of our society, these values can be reclaimed and rewoven into a transformed social order. That is the feminist agenda.

Cook summarized our challenge, our theory, and our basis for confidence, as follows:

> Revolution is a process and not an event. The power of women to come together, to support each other in community, in creative self-criticism and love, gives us the power to intensify the economic and political struggle. Wherever groups of women come together to define their own visions, economic and personal, and make connections with other groups of women working in our own interests, politically accountable to our own needs and wants, we are affirming a network of change. We are building the future.[38]

Our aim is not more and better jobs and services for women, but a feminist world. Unlike the man's world in which we presently live, however, ours offers the hopes of human liberation and of enabling people, in all their diversity, to become what they are capable of becoming, free of fear and exploitation. The feminist future is not for women only.

REFERENCES

1.   Julius Gould, "Ideology," in Gould and William Kolb, *A Dictionary of the Social Sciences* (New York: Free Press, 1964), p. 314.

2.   M. Ginsberg, in Julius Gould and William Kolb, *A Dictionary of the Social Sciences* (New York: Free Press, 1964), p. 317.

3.   Mary Bricker-Jenkins and Barbara Joseph, "Social Control and Social Change: Toward a Feminist Model of Social Work Practice." Paper presented at the NASW Conference on Social Work Practice in Sexist Society, Washington, D.C., 1980. (Mimeographed.)

4.   *Feminist Practice: Notes from the Tenth Year* (London, England: In Theory Press, 1979), p. 3.

5.   Barbara Demming, "Why Nonviolence?" in Bob Irwin and Gordon Faison, eds., *Newsletter of the Movement for a New Society* (Philadelphia: Movement for a New Society, undated), p. 4.

6.   Temma Kaplan, "Female Consciousness and Collective Action: The Case of Barcelona, 1910–1918," *Signs,* 7 (Spring 1982), pp. 545–566. See also Carol Gilligan, *In a Different Voice* (Cambridge, Mass.: Harvard University Press, 1981).

7.   Kaplan, "Female Consciousness and Collective Action," p. 546.

8.   Sharon Berlin, "Feminist Practice," p. 11. Paper presented at the Institute on Social Work Practice with Women, NASW Professional Symposium, Philadelphia, November 1981. (Mimeographed.)

9.   Zillah Eisenstein, "The Social Politics of the New Left: Understanding the 'Crisis of Liberalism' for the 1980's," *Signs,* 7 (Spring 1982), p. 569.

10.   See Linda Gordon and Allen Hunter, "Sex, Family, and the New Right: Antifeminism as a Political Force," *Radical America,* 11–12 (November 1977–February 1978); and Sheila Rowbotham, Lynn Segal, and Hilary Wainwright, *Beyond the Fragments: Feminism and the Making of Socialism* (Boston: Alyson Publications, 1981), pp. 157–209.

11.   Charlotte Bunch, "Women Power: The Courage to Lead, the Strength to Follow, and the Sense to Know the Difference," *Ms.* (July 1980), pp. 45–48; Cheryl Ellsworth et al., "Toward a Feminist Model of Planning," in Susan Vandiver and Ann Weick, *Women, Power, and Change* (Washington, D.C.: National Association of Social Workers, 1982), pp. 151–153; and Harstock, "Political Change: Two Perspectives of Power," *Building Feminist Theory: Essays from Quest* (New York: Longman, 1981), pp. 3–19.

12.   Barrie Thorne, "Review of *Building Feminist Theory: Essays from Quest,*" *Signs,* 7 (1982), p. 711.

13.   Ellsworth et al., "Toward a Feminist Model of Planning," succinctly summarizes the literature on process in feminist organizations. See also, Part 4, "Organizations and Strategies," in *Building Feminist Theory: Essays from Quest* (New York: Longman, 1981); and Rosalyn Baxandall, "Introduction to the U.S. Edition" of

Rowbotham, Segal, and Wainright, *Beyond the Fragments*, pp. ix–xvi. Lynne Segal, "A Local Experience," pp. 157–210, in Rowbotham, Segal, and Wainright points to process as the critical difference between feminist and most socialist theory and practice.

14. *Feminist Practice: Notes from the Tenth Year*, p. 3.

15. Joyce Rothschild-Whitt and Frank Lindenfeld, "Reshaping Work: Prospects and Problems of Workplace Democracy," in Lindenfeld and Rothschild-Whitt, eds., *Workplace, Democracy, and Social Change* (Boston: Porter Sargent, 1982), p. 17. See also George Dennison, "Politicizing of the Free School Movement," *New Schools Exchange Newsletter*, 77 (1972), pp. 2–3.

16. Rowbotham, Segal, and Wainright, *Beyond the Fragments*, pp. 177–180.

17. See Mary Bricker-Jenkins, "Organizing for Social Change and Transformation," paper presented at the Institute on Social Work Practice with Women, NASW National Symposium, Philadelphia, November 1981; and Marjorie Moskol, "Feminist Theory and Casework Practice," in Bernard Ross and S. K. Khinduka, eds., *Social Work in Practice* (Washington, D.C.: National Association of Social Workers, 1976), pp. 181–190.

18. Marge Piercy, "Contributions to Our Museum," *Living in the Open* (New York: Alfred A. Knopf, 1976), pp. 74–75.

19. Thus, for many feminists, capitalism, nationalism, and state socialism are, if not expressions of patriarchy, correlative systems that must be eliminated with it.

20. Ellsworth et al., "Toward a Feminist Model of Planning," pp. 151–153; Janice Wood Wetzel and the Feminist World View Educators, "Toward a Feminist World View Curriculum," paper presented at the Annual Program Meeting of the Council on Social Work Education, Fort Worth, Texas, March 1983, p. 10.

21. Michele Rosaldo, "The Use and Abuse of Anthropology: Reflections on Feminism and Cross-cultural Understanding," *Signs*, 5 (Spring 1980), pp. 389–417. See also Linda Nicholson, "Comment on Rosaldo. The Use and Abuse of Anthropology," *Signs*, 7 (Spring 1982), pp. 732–735.

22. Rothschild-Whitt and Lindenfeld, "Reshaping Work."

23. Editor's Note, "Special Issue on Feminist Theory," *Signs*, 7 (1982), p. 515.

24. Bricker-Jenkins, "Organizing for Social Change and Transformation"; and Bricker-Jenkins and Joseph, "Social Control and Social Change."

25. Mary Bricker-Jenkins, "Feminist Ideology and Organizations" (New York: Fordham University Graduate School of Social Services, 1983). (Mimeographed.)

26. Wood Wetzel and the Feminist World View Educators, "Toward a Feminist World View Curriculum."

27. Paolo Freire, "The Adult Literacy Process as Cultural Action for Freedom," *Harvard Educational Review*, 40 (1970), p. 205.

28. D. MacLeod and R. Bedard, "Women in Community," *Communities Magazine*, 25 (March–April 1977), p. 9.

29. Kate Lindemann, "A Feminist Method of Inquiry," p. 4. Unpublished paper, undated. (Mimeographed.)

30. Piercy, "Contributions to Our Museum," pp. 74–75.

31. The nature of the connections between interpersonal and social relationships is a topic of active dialogue in the feminist literature, although the existence of a connection is not in dispute. See, for example, Segal's comments on "the personal is political" in "A Local Experience," Rowbotham, Segal, and Wainwright, *Beyond the Fragments*, p. 198 ff.

32. Gordon and Hunter, "Sex, Family, and the New Left," as quoted in Rowbotham, Segal, and Wainright, *Beyond the Fragments*, pp. 154–155.

33. Thomas Lodahl and Stephen Mitchell, "Drift in the Development of Innovative Organizations," in John Kimberly, Robert Miles, and associates, *The Organizational Life Cycle* (San Francisco: Jossey-Bass, 1980), p. 186.

34. Blanche Wiesen Cook, *Women and Support Networks* (Brooklyn, N.Y.: Out and Out Books, 1979), p. 10.

35. Rothschild-Whitt and Lindenfeld, "Reshaping Work," p. 293.

36. Paolo Freire, "Research Methods," in John W. Ryan, ed., *Paolo Freire: Literacy Through Conscientization* (ERIC Documentation Series 114790, 1974), pp. 136–137. (Microfiche.)

37. Harry C. Boyte, *The Backyard Revolution* (Philadelphia: Temple University Press, 1980); John Case and Rosemary Taylor, *Coops, Communes, and Collectives* (New York: Pantheon Books, 1979); Marjorie Mayo, ed., *Women in the Community* (Boston: Routledge & Kegan Paul, 1977).

38. Cook, *Women and Support Networks*, p. 10.

PHANTASIA FOR ELVIRA SHATAYEV

*(leader of a women's climbing team, all of whom
died in a storm on Lenin Peak, August 1974. Later,
Shatayev's husband found and buried the bodies.)*

The cold felt cold until our blood
grew colder   then the wind
died down and we slept

If in this sleep I speak
it's with a voice no longer personal
(I want to say   *with voices*)
When the wind tore   our breath from us at last
we had no need of words
For months   for years   each one of us
had felt her own *yes*   growing in her
slowly forming   as she stood at windows   waited
For trains   mended her rucksack   combed her hair
What we were to learn   was simply   what we had
up here   as out of all words   that *yes*   had gathered
its forces   fused itself   and only just in time
to meet a *No* of no degrees
the black hole   sucking the world in

I feel you climbing toward me
your cleated bootsoles leaving   their geometric bite
colossally embossed   on microscopic crystals
as when I trailed you in the Caucasus

Now I am further
ahead   than either of us dreamed   anyone would be
I have become

the white snow packed like asphalt by the wind
the women I love   lightly flung   against the mountain
that blue sky
our frozen eyes unribboned   through the storm
we could have stitched that blueness   together   like a quilt

You come (I know this)   with your love   your loss
strapped to your body   with your tape-recorder   camera
ice-pick   against advisement
to give us burial in the snow   and in your mind
While my body lies out here
flashing like a prism   into your eyes
how could you sleep   You climbed here for yourself
we climbed for ourselves

When you have buried us   told your story
ours does not end   we stream
into the unfinished   the unbegun
the possible
Every cell's core of heat   pulsed out of us
into the thin air   of the universe
the armature of rock beneath these snows
this mountain   which has taken   the imprint of our minds
through changes elemental and minute
as those we underwent
to bring each other here
choosing ourselves   each other   and this life
whose every breath   and grasp   and further foothold
is somewhere   still enacted   and continuing

In the diary I wrote: *Now we are ready*
and each of us knows it   I have never loved
like this   I have never seen
my own forces so taken up and shared
and given back
After the long training   the early sieges
we are moving almost effortlessly in our love

In the diary as the wind   began to tear
at the tents over us   I wrote:
We know now we have always been in danger
down in our separateness
and now up here together   but till now
we had not touched our strength

In the diary torn from my fingers I had written:
What does love mean
what does it mean   "to survive"
A cable of blue fire ropes our bodies
burning together in the snow   We will not live
to settle for less   We have dreamed of this
all our lives

Adrienne Rich

From *The Dream of a Common Language, Poems 1974–1977*, by Adrienne Rich. Copyright © 1978 by W. W. Norton & Co. Reprinted by permission of the author and the publisher, W. W. Norton & Co.

Grounding the Definition of Feminist Practice

Mary Bricker-Jenkins
Nancy R. Hooyman

For feminist researchers, grounding theoretical formulations in experience is a challenge and a commitment. An examination of the literature from the contemporary feminist movement reported in the previous chapter yielded important insights about the ideological underpinnings of feminist practice. However, the authors wished to examine more directly the experience of social workers who identified themselves as feminist to "ground" the definition of feminist practice in that experience. The empirical work of the Feminist Practice Project emerged from this commitment. This chapter is based on the results of the 1983-84 pilot study for the research currently in progress. ——Editor's Note

The pilot study was sponsored by the National Committee on Women's Issues (NCOWI) of the National Association of Social Workers (NASW) as part of its effort to identify, develop, and disseminate information about feminist social work practice.[1] Fifty packets, each containing three sets of project descriptions and questionnaires, were distributed to social work educators and practitioners at the 1983 Annual Program Meeting of the Council on Social Work Education. The only criteria for inclusion in the survey were the respondents' definitions of themselves as feminist practitioners and their willingness to complete a lengthy questionnaire that contained many open-ended items.

Persons who volunteered to take a packet were asked to distribute two of the three questionnaires to colleagues in their community. Of the 150 survey instruments distributed in this manner, 36 were returned, for a 24 percent response rate. Given the small number of respondents, the method of distribution (which was dictated by cost factors), and the exploratory nature of the effort, the findings must be considered tentative. Intended for use as "grounding" for the development of a more sensitive instrument and research study, a content analysis of these responses revealed only the boundaries and contours of the terrain; the sketching in of important details must await further investigation.

PRACTITIONERS AND THEIR WORK

All the respondents were engaged at least part time in some form of direct practice in a wide variety of settings. The greatest concentrations were in mental health, in services related to violence against women, and in education. (Educators regarded their work as their practice, but also were active in their communities on other issues.) Of the 36 responses, 33 came from persons who held a professional social work degree and 3 were from "other human service professionals." Of these 3, 1 was a DSW candidate and 2 held doctorates in related fields but were working in social work jobs.

Many were involved in providing services to women whose concerns had been defined in new ways through the agitation, advocacy, and research of feminists. These concerns and problems included battering, rape, incest, displaced homemakers, women's studies, alternative families, and older women. Nearly all the respondents were engaged in attempts to gain recognition of the special needs of women and to develop services to meet them. Many were involved in issues that directly affect all persons, such as peace and disarmament and racism, but they brought a uniquely feminist consciousness and definition of the problems to these issues.

The infusion of feminist consciousness into all aspects of their work took many forms, as did the related concept of seeing the personal as political. To make services accessible to all women, practitioners not only offered sliding scales but were often willing to barter their services. Many combined private practice with "public" practice. When engaged in research, practitioners were feminizing the process, asking new questions, modifying the methodologies, and assuming a clear advocacy posture. Going beyond such common notions of "political social work" as advocacy and engagement in the legislative process, the feminist practitioners usually encouraged their clients to become involved in political action, often at their side; to engage with them as collaborators in the provision of services; to make explicit their value stance toward social change; and to identify and attempt to confront the political dimensions in all social transactions, ranging from the client's experience with social institutions to the practice contract and the helping relationship.

DEFINITION OF FEMINIST PRACTICE

We did not provide a definition of feminist practice to the participants, opting instead to allow them to define themselves as feminist practitioners and to permit the meaning of "feminist" and "feminist practice" to emerge from the responses. What evolved was a picture of practice that would clearly fall within any broad definition of social work practice (such as that of Bartlett or the widely used definition by Pincus and Minahan), but with certain identifiable emphases.[2] In general, feminist practitioners do the following:

■ Approach all issues presented by social living and social relationships with a view to identifying their implications for women.

- Are concerned with the ways in which patterns of institutionalized sexism (and, usually, other oppressive ideologies and behaviors) create problems for all persons and for women in particular.
- Are committed to the development of specific actions and techniques to remove barriers, both material and ideological, to the fullest possible development of the abilities of individuals and groups.
- Tend to view social work practice as a "political" practice, that is, as a normatively based and directed effort to enable people to control the conditions of their lives by moving power distributions in a more egalitarian direction.

CHARACTERISTICS OF PRACTICE

Although we did not offer a definition of feminist practice, we derived a list of characteristics ("qualities and emphases") that had been suggested in the literature on feminist theory as being characteristic of feminist practice in general. Respondents were asked to indicate which they felt were reflected in their social work practice. All the characteristics were confirmed by a majority of those who responded to this section of the questionnaire (only 32 of the 36 completed this section); the number of "not sure" responses on two of the items, however, was high enough to warrant further clarification. These were "praxis" (theory-practice) orientation and "preference for collectivism." Because both these terms were derived from socialist-feminist literature, it is not surprising that they received stronger confirmation in responses that were categorized as "radical" than those that were considered "liberal-reformist."

The characteristics, in descending order of confirmation, were as follows: the use of consciousness-raising techniques or goals; an emphasis on process; the use of networking, support, and self-help groups; the valuing of diversity; an emphasis on egalitarian relationships and mutuality; an emphasis on women's experience; the valuing of multidimensional thinking and analysis; an emphasis on empowerment; an orientation to social, political, or economic change; an explicitly political-normative-ideological orientation; an emphasis on basic needs and objective conditions; a preference for consensus–democratic decision making; an orientation to "praxis" (theory/practice); and a preference for "collectivism."

Many other characteristics were suggested by the respondents. Most appeared to be a rephrasing with different elaborations of those listed, with one exception. An emphasis on renaming reality and the elimination of sexist language was listed by many respondents in different ways.

DEFINITIONS OF PROBLEMS, GOALS, AND METHODS

As noted earlier, a distinguishing feature of feminist practice noted by the respondents was a consistent belief in the societal or cultural origins of the distress experienced by their clients; as one respondent put it, "I focus on the environment, the dynamics of oppression, and disempowerment in all situations." Another response also reflected the voices of many: "Women are an emergent group looking for grounding in all areas of power and influence. The problems we face are ones of culture and the good of the powerful. . . . I see over and over again the effects of tradition, acculturation, and dependency."

Given this emphasis on the public and political dimensions of problems and issues, feminist practitioners saw their work, at least in part, as oriented to the goals of social change. Moreover, these practitioners would not be contained by common notions of what is reasonable and possible in social efforts. Typical statements included "abolish prisons as we know them"; "transform the workplace"; "create new family structures"; "eliminate racism, sexism, homophobia, and heterosexism"; "eliminate war"; "change the welfare system and the economic structure of society"; "direct benefit, improve the position of women; indirect benefit, improve the position of all oppressed people." There is a slogan in the popular women's movement, "Nothing is impossible!" Feminist practitioners apparently believe it and derive strength and vision from this belief.

Precisely how practitioners explicate the underlying and implicit theory of social change and link their goals for social change to their work with individual clients and groups is a rich area for further investigation. Some patterns, however, can be identified from the respondents' answers on the questionnaires. For example, the respondents emphasized empowerment through the teaching of problem-solving, interpersonal, and life-management skills and through participation in collective action. Their use of consciousness-raising techniques to unmask the cultural origins of distress led to the idea that "there are no private solutions to collective problems" (a point emphasized by many respondents) and to the search for a common ground among women and their issues. This idea, in turn, led to collective action of some sort in the majority of cases. "Starting from an individual approach," as one respondent described the process, "the movement toward collective action becomes self-evident."

Ideas of what constitutes collective action are linked to ideas about what is "political." Many definitions were given, but the common theme in all of them was that "political" referred to the distribution of power in all social systems, from the family to the society at large, and was not narrowly construed to refer only to formal public processes. Thus, although some of the respondents' activities were directed to these processes, such as work in the electoral and legislative processes, use of the courts, or advocacy in professional organizations, the respondents also heavily emphasized grass-roots organization and activism.

To the respondents, collective action frequently meant building and engaging in coalitions, but these coalitions often took on a unique cast that was consonant with the valuing of diversity linked with notions of common ground and the value of grass-roots work. For example, one respondent stated: "The powerful are not the allies; rather, I build coalitions of the disempowered." This same approach was evidenced in work with smaller social systems, such as families and work groups. Speaking of her work in a health care setting, a respondent said: "I attempt to find and work from the common ground of the client, the client's family, and the workers, all of whom are victims of an inadequate and sometimes exploitative health care system."

Because the helping relationship is itself political, the respondents emphasized the creation of a relationship structure that would provide clients with opportunities to experience the move from dependence to power and control over their own lives. Often the clients accomplished this goal through increased participation in groups, which were characterized by mutuality and supportiveness as well as the expectation that the clients would assume personal responsibility.

In seeking social change, the respondents attempted to identify and reclaim those aspects of women's individual and collective experience that have been hidden and devalued. They began to do so by "breaking the silence," which enables the discovery of a common ground and establishes publicly the uniqueness and diversity of women's experiences. A respondent likened the situation of women to that of native people in the Arctic: "They are fighting multinational corporations and world powers to preserve their uniqueness, languages, and so forth. They want to participate in the arenas of power but won't compromise who they are. Women must behave in consonant ways."

To summarize, feminist practice, as described by our respondents, is usually *generalist* in approach, with both assessment and intervention techniques encompassing the range of potential focal points on the continuum of private troubles to public issues. It usually incorporates consciousness raising and educational techniques selected to foster empowerment of the client and often encourages engagement by the client (sometimes with the practitioner) in social and political action for its potential therapeutic as well as social-change value. Attempts are made by the practitioner to "depathologize" practice by avoiding labels and by focusing on specific strengths that have evolved from women's attempts to deal with oppressive circumstances. Diversity and uniqueness also are protected and promoted through the conscious inclusion of such influences as ethnicity, class, sexual orientation, and the like in determining approaches with the client; in organizing efforts, diversity is viewed as a source of strength. Attempts are also made to demystify the helping process by providing information and encouraging the client's assumption of responsibility. The preference is for an egalitarian, collaborative working relationship with the client. For this and other reasons, there is heavy reliance on the use of groups and support networks, as well as on coalitions in political work. There is generally an explicit value and ethical stance that is consciously used to motivate and evaluate practice. Although all practice embodies such a stance, feminist practice is distinguished by its conscious effort to achieve congruence of goals, process, and structure with its values and ethics.

VARIATIONS ON FEMINIST PRACTICE

Many variations of practice were discernible in the responses, the number and type depending on the dimensions of practice on which one chose to focus in analyzing the open-ended responses. Those that seemed immediate and compelling were related to the respondents' political orientation and to certain demographic variables, but the categories derived from the data must be considered tentative, fluid, and overlapping.[3] We present them because they convey a richness of diversity, which confounds our efforts to define the field and compels further efforts to discover its many features.

Differences in Political Orientation

In examining the material on statements of goals and definitions of problems, the differences in political orientation were evident. These differences were carried through the descriptions of activities and methods used in practice. Because of a lack of originality and in acknowledgment of our imprecision, we labeled the groups "liberal/reformist" and "radical"; the respondents were fairly evenly divided between the two groups.[4] Both groups share the view that women have been systematically denied opportunities and choices, particularly in the family and the workplace. Liberal-reformist practitioners tend to see this process as being linked to sexist socialization and acculturation patterns and thus view practice primarily in terms of resocialization and reeducation. They consider that the political implications are for the society in general. These implications include the need for such reforms as affirmative action, additional and more sensitive services for women, a redefinition of sex and gender roles, and opportunities for interpersonal skills and enhanced self-esteem based on a positive evaluation of women and women's experience. As one respondent put it, her work "furthers the notion that society has oppressed women, oppression is wrong, and that the healthiest part of a woman is her refusal to conform. I help displaced homemakers, the new poor, lesbians, and blacks claim their place in society." There is generally an assumption that the necessary reforms can take place within the context of the current social order "as revised."

Although the two groups agreed on many issues, and the distinctions between the groups were not rigid, radical feminists seek a more fundamental transformation of the social order based on a different set of values and assumptions about human needs and human nature. They view problems in relation to structures and ideologies and goals in terms of changing them. As one respondent put it: "The primary issues are oppression and acceptance of differences.... The goal of practice is to create social, political, and economic structures which enable self-actualization and empowerment for all." This analysis directs a practice that is more heavily oriented to taking control of resources, creating opportunities for choice, and emphasizing political action and organizing to achieve these goals.

Demographic Characteristics

In addition to variations based on political orientation, there also were indications of variations based on certain demographic characteristics. Three characteristics that stood out were race and ethnicity, sexual orientation, and geography (residence in a rural versus an urban area). This pattern would suggest that socioeconomic class, age, gender, and other characteristics also influence the ways in which the practitioner elaborates the feminist perspective in her work. Given the emphasis on diversity in feminist practice, it is not surprising that we found attempts to practice the intersection of race, class, and gender or of gender and sexual preference or of myriad other combinations of identities that have profound effects on the ways in which we view ourselves and our worlds. Althought the respondents indicated that these "demographic variables" (for lack of a better term) often compelled differential development and application of the feminist perspective, the specific nature of the differences requires much more investigation and analysis. What can be said now is this: If feminist theory provides the lens through which the world is viewed, political and demographic characteristics influence the specific qualities of the lens and in some cases may compel the development of an entirely new one.

Psychic-Physical Healer Perspective

Another variation of feminist practice, which stands by itself and defies categorization, is the psychic–physical healer perspective. This variation emerges from the efforts of some feminists to integrate physical and spiritual dimensions into practice and to reclaim and use ancient healing arts practiced by women. Examples of such healing arts and techniques include imaging, psychic healing, meditation, massage and other body work, rituals, and spiritualism. Usually shunned by mainstream professionals who are oriented to rational scientific endeavors, these methods and techniques are nevertheless widely used by many feminists who are committed to them. Thus, it is not surprising to find feminist social workers developing practice based on a synthesis of these techniques and social work methods. As one respondent said, some feminist social workers are integrating these techniques with their "knowledge of human behavior in general and [specific knowledge of] the effects of individual, family, and cultural scripting."

THEORETICAL AND CULTURAL BASE OF FEMINIST PRACTICE

To find the commonly chosen theoretical sources, we asked the respondents to list the most significant influences on their work. Many listed experiential influences, such as participation in the women's movement, feminist friends, personal therapy, and their mothers.

Of the published works, however, only a few were mentioned more than once or twice. They included writing by such contemporary feminist theoreticians as Betty Friedan (usually specifying her "early" work), Anne Wilson Schaef, Mary Daly, Robin Morgan, Andrea Dworkin, and Susan Brownmiller. A few "foremothers" were mentioned, including Emma Goldman and Charlotte Perkins Gilman. Among social and behavioral scientists, only Jean Baker Miller and Carol Gilligan were noted more than once, but Gilligan's theory of the moral development of women has apparently been widely discussed.[5] The only social worker who was mentioned more than once was Bertha Reynolds, although many cited as catalytic the 1980 NASW Conference on Social Work Practice in Sexist Society.

The most remarkable finding related to the influences on feminist practice was this: Mentioned twice as often as any other influence, and cited by at least 20 percent of the respondents, were women musicians (especially Holly Near, Meg Christian, and Chris Williamson), feminist poets (primarily Marge Piercy, Ann Sexton, Adrienne Rich, and Audre Lorde), and the cooperatively produced art work of Judy Chicago. The specific ways in which practitioners incorporate these influences in their practice warrants further investigation, but, once again, these influences suggest the power of symbolism and its role in creating alternative cultural and political realities. They suggest the recognition that our culture expresses our theory in ways which cannot be captured by the social sciences alone and that this recognition must be incorporated into our practice.

Feminist practice, rooted in an alternative cultural system that reflects and reinforces women's reality, as distinguished from that of the dominant culture, requires for its evolution structures, symbols, and methods that are consonant with its values, assumptions, and material bases. The creation of this culture is what feminist practice ultimately is about.

REFERENCES

1. After the pilot study, NCOWI was awarded a grant from the NASW Program Advancement Fund to continue the work of the project. During 1984–85, we engaged in qualitative research to enlarge our understanding of feminist practice. When funds become available, we will undertake a national mail survey of feminist practitioners.

2. Harriett M. Bartlett, *The Common Base of Social Work Practice* (New York: National Association of Social Workers, 1970), pp. 63–152; and Allen Pincus and Ann Minahan, *Social Work Practice: Model and Method* (Itasca, Ill.: F. E. Peacock Publishers, 1973), p. 9. See also Scott Briar, "Social Work Practice: Contemporary Issues," *Encyclopedia of Social Work* (Washington, D.C.: National Association of Social Workers, 1977), pp. 1529–1534.

3. Many feminist researchers warn that the emphasis on categorization in positivist research tends to obscure much of the diversity of the phenomenological world and masks significant idiosyncrasies.

4.   Because the number of respondents was small and the instrument was not designed to detail differences among them, we grouped respondents who reflected a socialist orientation with those whose remarks suggested other radical perspectives. Although they differed in analysis and strategy, these respondents shared an interest in developing alternatives to the liberal/reformist approach.

5.   Carol Gilligan, *In a Different Voice* (Cambridge, Mass.: Harvard University Press, 1982); and Jean Baker Miller, *Toward a New Psychology of Women* (Boston: Beacon Press, 1976).

AND THEN ALL THAT HAS DIVIDED US

And then all that has divided us will merge
And then compassion will be wedded to power
And then softness will come to a world that is harsh and unkind
And then both men and women will be gentle
And then both women and men will be strong
And then no person will be subject to another's will
And then all will be rich and free and varied
And then the greed of some will give way to the needs of many
And then all will share equally in the Earth's abundance
And then all will care for the sick and the weak and the old
And then all will nourish the young
And then all will cherish life's creatures
And then all will live in harmony with each other and the Earth
And then everywhere will be called Eden once again

JUDY CHICAGO

From *The Dinner Party* by Judy Chicago. Copyright © 1979 by Judy Chicago. Reprinted by permission of the author and the publisher, Doubleday & Co.

Reformist Feminism

I WANT YOU TO GIVE ME SOME MONEY

I want you to give me some money,
Because you have a job you love and will
continue to love.
I can see you
riding that sweet red tractor
steady
almost perfect
even when you're looking backward.
You have work you love
on the land
we both love
and
came to
together—
teenagers,
just married.
You showed me things
about how to love land
just plain dirt and grass,
weeds
trees.
You quizzed me on names of friends I have now
like Sorrell
Lamb's Quarters
and Honeysuckle hiding a nest of Mockingbird eggs.
I watched you plant things to eat
and I decided I would plant too
but I wouldn't eat them.
I would sit and look at them.
I would putter around from one to the other and smile
at them and wish them good morning
while drinking coffee
before running
exactly one mile.
I can still see those first Zinnias
opening my heart with their crimson
fat
beauty.

And golden Marigolds,
Daylilies
Daisies, a Daffodil—
all standing there
haughty and strong,
cradling me
under the wide
blue sky
of
my secret oppression.

Chorus:
What is clear
to me now
is you got more
than I did
and
I gave more than you.
This is the truth.
So give me some money.

I want you to give me some money.
because I stayed with you
too long.
So long
that now my
reasoned remorse tugs inside me at negation
of
my life.
Negation of those years we were both working
raising that blond-headed
blue-eyed
big-smiling
boy
child.
Me
arranging minimally reasonable daycare
organizing
all those
logistics
worrying
guiding
thinking
counseling
wondering
how long this could last.

How long could I last
doing things like
Thursday afternoons
after work
dividing tasks
explaining
you do
the vacuuming
the dishes
the bathroom
and I'll do all
the rest
because I want it a certain way.
tidy.
no dust.
anywhere.

I want you to give me some money
because of all those years you were
hurting me.
And when I said
this hurts
you said
no it doesn't
and I said
oh
I thought it did
and went on
thinking I shouldn't be hurting,
feeling bad
I was hurting.
Feeling crazy that I wanted
a different feeling, a different life
than what I had.

I want you to give me some money
because you're a white man
and you have enough power
as it is
and I
deserve
some time of stretching
of freedom
of figuring more things out
about how to live this life
about how to furnish this home.
This is really my home.
This is finally my home.
And I want you to give me some money
for it.

LYNDA LOU EASE

A Reformist Perspective on Feminist Practice

Linda Stere

The author describes how she combines private practice and public practice to advance the cause of women. Her preference for the use of groups is based on feminist values, empowers women, and dilutes the vitiating experience of "experts." She describes the techniques she uses with individuals, groups, and families (including lesbian couples) to enhance self-esteem, enable the expression of anger, and foster the ability to engage in conflict resolution. Questions are raised about the sexist assumptions under-pinning most assertiveness training ("masculinity training for women"), and alternative methods are discussed. Similar investigations are suggested of the sexist and heterosexist theory and assumptions lurking in much, if not most, mental health and social ser-vice practice. ——Editor's Note

I am a self-employed clinical social worker in Nashville, Tennessee. I hesitate to use the term "private practice" because it connotes a certain style of self-employed practice that does not reflect the feminist values and ac-tivities that clinically and economically guide both the private and public aspects of my work.

I consider my practice to be feminist in that my interventions, which are intended to serve better the needs of women, include the regular offering of women's groups and workshops for networking and skill building, orga-nizing all-women self-help groups and therapy groups, charging fees on a sliding scale, doing therapy with lesbian couples with a woman cotherapist, providing information and referral services for women, and using models for social and personal intervention that are based on the developing theories about women. I also feel a responsibility to reach out to women through

Linda Stere, MSW, is a self-employed practitioner in Nashville, Tennessee. She has co-chaired the Committee on Women's Issues of the Tennessee Chapter of NASW and has taught courses on women and treatment at the University of Tennessee School of Social Work. Her article, "Feminist Assertiveness Training: Self-Esteem Groups as Skill Training for Women," appears in Lynne Bravo Rosewater and Lenore E. A. Walker, eds., Handbook of Feminist Therapy: Women's Issues in Psychotherapy, *published by Springer Publishing Co., New York, 1985.*

community programs, such as the YWCA personal growth program and emergency shelter service, and to social work colleagues, through regular continuing education programs to improve services to women sponsored by the Women's Issues Committee of the NASW Tennessee Chapter.

In speaking to a class of graduate social work students in a treatment relationship seminar, I was naively surprised to learn that most students in that all-woman class were hesitant to show an interest in feminism. I surmised that their stereotypes of and their lack of knowledge of the principles of feminist practice prevented them from seeing how feminist methodology and practice dovetail with the basic values and practice of social work. In the past, much of what is valuable in social work has, at times, been lost in the profession's efforts to conform to other helping professions that are more prestigious than ours; in doing so, we social workers have sacrificed the strengths and uniqueness of our profession. Feminism brings the social worker back to practices rooted in the humanistic and ecological perspectives. Feminist practice also offers a specific conceptual framework for examining the expression and interplay of and the conflict between masculine and feminine values in our various cultures, individuals, and families.

Certainly, feminist practice that focuses solely on the needs of women without considering the systemic effects of change is easily criticized. A skilled feminist social worker, however, like any effective social worker, remains constantly aware of and thoughtfully weighs the consequences of change for all levels of the system—the individual, the family, the community, and society.

ASSERTIVENESS TRAINING VERSUS SELF-ESTEEM TRAINING

In doing feminist practice, we must continuously examine our work for possible sexist errors. This article discusses the skill training groups I offer to women, which I call "self-esteem training." These groups are a revision of the assertiveness training groups I formerly offered that were based on assertiveness training books written by women and for women. In the past few years, several feminist researcher-behaviorists have examined the possible pitfalls in assertiveness training. They have questioned whether such training may provide yet another means for women to devalue themselves in their search to copy a masculine style of assertiveness.[1] As frequently practiced, assertiveness training groups could be described as "masculinity-training" groups in which women are taught direct, concise, "rational" methods of conveying messages and learn a "bill of individual rights" that may lead to feelings of inadequacy for having a keen sensitivity to others. Although assertiveness training groups have provided an invaluable path and alternative for women who want to expand themselves, many extremely feminine women, who suffer most from the role constraints of passivity and submissiveness, often drop out of training groups whose messages are too dystonic to their way of being.[2]

Self-esteem training, by contrast, is a valuable tool to bring to women who ascribe to extreme sex-role patterns and who have low self-esteem. It also can be a positive, strength-building approach for all groups of women who seek to improve their sense of self-respect and self-worth. Many of the exercises and methods used in self-esteem training can be done in groups or with individuals. However, the group mode is preferable because it offers the opportunity to dilute the "expert" status of the social worker, to alleviate distress that arises primarily from being isolated from the experiences of other women, and to provide a means for empowering women by encouraging them to help one another.

Positive helping methods, which focus on assessing and supporting clients' inner resources, rather than on classifying their deficits through diagnoses of pathology, are being more widely practiced and respected. This change in orientation is especially significant for women whose culturally inferior status has traditionally been reflected and reinforced by the helping professions.[3] Self-esteem training is a resource-focused approach that, when done comprehensively, becomes much more than a primer of "positive thinking" methods. It becomes an opportunity to reframe women's "weaknesses" as strengths to direct them to their internal resources rather than to "appropriate behavior," and to validate their experiences, needs, and feelings through sharing with other women.[4] Frequently, the improvement in self-esteem is considered to be an indirect effect of other training procedures, such as assertiveness training, or is deemed too general or too vague a concept to be approached behaviorally. Many of the techniques described later in this article are so obvious and simple that we may forget to utilize them as we search for more esoteric methods for change. The aim of my work is to encourage women to follow their instinctive urges to practice these direct positive techniques and to validate the importance of such activities in social work.

Conducting a self-esteem training group can be an enjoyable, rewarding, and enduring experience, as the following example illustrates.

> The group began with a large enrollment in a YWCA personal growth program. Although 18 members could be an unwieldy number for a group of such short duration (four to six meetings), a well-structured format and the conduct of most exercises in small subgroups of 2 to 4 women provided the opportunity for more intimate sharing. As early as the second meeting, women were sharing personal and at times painful aspects of their lives, which demonstrates the often rapid cohesiveness of all-women groups.
>
> The large group also was able to accommodate a range of differences in background, interests, and current life problems. Some of the women had significant psychiatric treatment, including hospitalization, while others had received none at all, avoiding one-to-one therapy. For some women, the group was more like an educational experience, while for other women, the group so moved them that their deeply suppressed feelings were aroused. All styles of involvement were accepted and affirmed, and the differences were framed as various expressions of their common experience.

At the conclusion of the training group, as in most groups, the women were invited to participate in an ongoing support group. Eight women exchanged addresses and telephone numbers and began meeting weekly; they asked the facilitator to join them every other week for more focused personal work. This group evolved into a self-support group for middle-aged women, and it continues three years later to be, according to its members, a significant therapeutic experience. Although the knowledge of self-esteem skills and the guidelines for personal change were reported to be interesting materials, evaluations from this group, as in most training groups, showed that it is the healing effect of sharing personal experiences with other women that has the most significant impact.

SKILLS

In Table 1, the skills of self-esteem training are presented under four major headings. Defining the goals of personal growth in terms of discreet substeps provides a workable path for change—one that seems accessible and achievable to the group members who often have stated their goals in such general terms as "liking myself" or "having more confidence." Note that the four skills are subdivided into thinking, feeling, and action components.

Each of the 12 specific subgoals can be used as a theme for an in-depth discussion or a personal evaluation and can be illustrated and practiced through specific exercises.[5] To be effective, self-esteem training should integrate several social work approaches, namely, feminist, behavioral, and task centered. Skill building in self-esteem training does not have primarily an interpersonal focus as it does in assertiveness training, but, rather, centers on the woman's inner dialogue and on enhancing her relationship to herself. Helping each woman to see that she is responsible for herself, just as she feels a responsibility to others, is a significant first step toward building self-respect.

EXERCISES

Exercises appropriate to the subgoals listed in Table 1 could be categorized as techniques in strength building, cognitive restructuring, and relaxation. The following summary of exercises was adapted from a rich array of resources.[6] Readers are encouraged to be creative in selecting cognitive, affective, and behavioral exercises for group work. Group members are typically given a variety of suggestions for homework, which indicates that there is no one best exercise for all and that women must respect their uniqueness in selecting tasks for themselves.

Strength-Building Exercises

Self-appreciation list. Have the group member complete at least six phrases to herself, such as "I like my...," "I appreciate my...," "I am pleased with the way I...," "I am proud of...." She can include qualities accomplishments, interests, and abilities. Ask how she felt doing so.

Table 1. Skills of Self-Esteem Training

Accepting My Feelings as Rational and Valid

Validating my feelings of guilt and resentment by tracing their
sources; recognizing that having strong feelings does not
necessarily mean being out of control
Trusting that my feeling reactions are my genuine and unique
response to something real.
Being able to express my feelings to others as I so choose.

Being Able to Please Myself

Knowing what I like, want, and need.
Feeling important and worthy enough to say what I want.
Taking action in my own behalf; making requests.

Identifying My Strengths

Revealing my feminine skills and qualities.
Feeling the courage to be as successful and capable as I can be.
Making positive statements about myself to myself and others.

Knowing and Accepting My Imperfections and Being Gentle With Myself

Having realistic expectations of myself and manageable ideals to
inspire me.
Feeling calm in the face of criticism.
Being able to state my shortcomings.

From Linda Stere, "Feminist Assertiveness Training: Self-Esteem Groups as Skill Training for Women" in Lynne Bravo Rosewater and Lenore E. A. Walker, eds., *Handbook of Feminist Therapy: Women's Issues in Psychotherapy.* Copyright © 1985 by Springer Publishing Co. Reprinted by permission of the publisher.

Admiration list. Have her list three women she admires or appreciates (relatives, famous contemporary women, friends, fictional women, historical figures). Next, have her list after each name what she appreciates about each one. Then relate these qualities to qualities she possesses or aspires to have.

Life successes. Divide her life span into age segments (of five to ten years each). Under each period, have her list memories, accomplishments, people, and events about which she feels good.

Compliments exercise. In dyads or in triads, using an observer and the self-appreciation list, have the woman hand her list to her partner or partners to review. The partner, glancing at the list each time, phrases the self-likes in her own words and compliments the woman, with enthusiasm and feeling, as if she had known her a long time. The woman is to accept the compliment verbally with a brief phrase of "thank you." The observer's role is to note eye contact and how the woman received the compliments, giving her feedback at the end and inquiring how she felt during the exercise. This exercise should first be modeled.

Boasting exercise. In groups of four or more, have each woman use her self-appreciation list as a resource. As she stands in front of the other women, she should engage in expressive bragging or boasting about herself. She is coached to "sell herself" by maintaining a grounded posture and good eye contact. After each woman finishes (in three to five minutes), the rest are coached to applaud her enthusiastically. After the exercise, review how each woman felt. This exercise should first be modeled.

Cognitive-Restructuring Exercises

Awareness of negative self-talk. Have the group member keep for two weeks a daily journal of her criticisms or warnings to herself. Review her reaction to doing so and examine the reality of each statement. If she cannot do this exercise, go on to the next one.

Shoulds-resentments list. Categorize aspects of her life into several relevant categories (mother, wife, daughter, friend, worker, homemaker, and so on). Have her list under each one the negative messages she gives herself by completing the phrase "I should (be)...." Discuss and explore the guilt and anger fueled by these negative thoughts. Then ask her to translate the negative self-statements into positive ones or at least into an honest desire for change by completing the phrases, "I really am...," or "I want to be more...."

Positive self-talk. This exercise is a thought-stopping technique for negative ruminating or panic-arousing thoughts. Instruct and model for the woman how to talk out loud to herself in a slow, calm, reassuring manner by completing such sentences as "It isn't so bad if...." "It's not the end of the world if...." "You really can survive...." "You didn't do badly at...." In each case, she states the positive "facts" of the situation until she has convinced herself and her level of panic drops.

List of personal rights. Using any popular assertion-training book as a resource, create with the woman a list of basic human rights (for example, "you have a right to make mistakes" or "you have a right to change your mind"). Explore how she deprives herself of these rights. Have her state them out loud to you.

Examining irrational beliefs. Ask her to check which beliefs she knows she holds, even if intellectually she questions such beliefs. The process of questioning and refuting such beliefs helps her deal with expectations of perfection in the world and in herself.

Relaxation Techniques

Journaling. Ask the group member to keep a notebook handy to record daily or whenever she is moved to write, her thoughts, feelings, reflections, and dialogues with herself about her reactions to events, people, dreams, and the like. This technique is useful in dealing with deep feelings (anger or grief) or in unraveling confusion and uncertainty.

Exercise-activity. Have her list several activities that she enjoys doing. She can post a list of distracting activities to turn to as a thought–worry–stopping technique. The benefits of walking, jogging, or exercise classes at least three times a week should be presented.

Sensory focusing. To help her redirect her attention from anxious rehearsal of the past or future to the present, have her make a list of several activities involving the senses of seeing, listening, smelling, tasting, and touching that give her pleasure. Coach her to attend fully to these activities, savoring this experience instead of ruminating (for example, listening to a favorite record, looking at scenery while driving, tasting slowly a favorite food, savoring the smells of a spring walk, and enjoying the feel of digging the dirt in a garden).

Muscle-relaxation exercises. Teach her to focus internally instead of externally and show her she can have control over her inner anxiety through practice in breathing and concentrating. If these meditation-type exercises are not helpful, direct her to more active ones (exercise and activity).

REFERENCES

1. See Iris G. Fodor and R. C. Epstein, "Assertiveness Training for Women: Where Are We Failing?" in Paul Emmelkamp and Edna Foa, eds., *Failures in Behavior Therapy* (New York: John Wiley & Sons, 1983); and Sharon E. Kahn, "Issues in the Assessment and Training of Assertiveness with Women," in Jeri D. Wine and Marti D. Smye, eds., *Social Competence* (New York: Guilford, 1981). See also, M. Linehan and K. Egan, "Assertion Training for Women: Square Peg in a Round Hole?" Paper presented at the Symposium on Behavioral Therapy for Women, Annual Meeting of the Association of Advanced Behavior Therapy, San Francisco, California, 1979.

2. Elizabeth M. Ellis and Michael P. Nichols, "A Comparative Study of Feminist and Traditional Group Assertiveness Training with Women," *Psychotherapy: Theory, Research, and Practice,* 4 (1979), pp. 467–474.

3. See Elaine Norman, "Sex Roles and Sexism," and Gloria Donadello, "Women and the Mental Health System," in Norman and Arline Mancuso, eds., *Women's Issues and Social Work Practice* (Itasca, Ill.: F. E. Peacock Publishers, 1980). See also, Janice Wood Wetzel, "Redefining Concepts of Mental Health," in Ann Weick and Susan T. Vandiver, eds., *Women, Power, and Change* (Washington, D.C.: National Association of Social Workers, 1982), pp. 3–16.

4. See Jean Baker Miller, *Toward a New Psychology of Women* (Boston: Beacon Press, 1976).

5. For a more detailed description of the structure of and clinical guidelines for these training groups, see Linda Stere, "Feminist Assertiveness Training: Self-Esteem

Groups as Skill Training for Women," in Lynne Bravo Rosewater and Lenore E. A. Walker, eds., *Handbook of Feminist Therapy: Women's Issues in Psychotherapy*: (New York: Springer Publishing Co., 1985), pp. 31–79.

6. Many exercises were adapted from the confidence-building sections of assertiveness training books, such as Stanlee Phelps and Nancy Austin, *The Assertive Woman* (San Luis Obispo, Calif.: Impact, 1975): Colleen Kelley, *Assertion Training: A Facilitator's Guide* (La Jolla, Calif.: University Associates, 1979); Susan M. Osborn and Gloria G. Harris, *Assertive Training for Women* (Springfield, Ill.: Charles C. Thomas, 1975); and from Dorothy Jongward and Dru Scott, *Women as Winners* (Reading, Mass.: Addison-Wesley Publishing Co., 1976).

THE ROCK WILL WEAR AWAY

For someone who usually composes in total isolation, never uttering a public peep until every note, every word is perfectly polished and practiced, the experience of co-writing a song was fairly traumatic But it was real wonderful to learn to share creative processes, and then to even like the result!

The theme of the chorus is a common one: many small, weak entities joining together to defeat a larger, stronger one. Holly heard the rock water imagery in a Vietnamese poem, while I fondly recall the flies in the elephant's nose in Judy Grahn's poem. You haven't really heard this song until you've sung it yourself with a whole roomful of women. For me, that experience is one of those moments when I feel our growing collective strength and purpose, and I know we can win.

Sixteen-year-old virgin
Springtime takes her to the park
Where the moon shines down like the future calling her out of the dark
But her nightmare finds her freedom
And leaves her lying wounded, worn from invasion

Light as a feather floating by
Landing, then covered with soot
Waiting now, watching now for rain
To wash clean her pain

CHORUS:

Can we be like drops of water falling on the stone
Splashing, breaking, dispersing in air
Weaker than the stone by far
But be aware that as time goes by
The rock will wear away
And the water comes again

Thirty-year-old mother
Autumn finds her pregnant once more
And the leaves like gold and copper reminding her that she is poor
And her children often are hungry
And she hungers too, for knowledge, time and choices

CHORUS:

Eighty-year-old poet
Winter keeps her home and alone
Where she freezes and darkness keeps her from writing her final wisdom
But she lights her last red candle
And as it is melting, tilting it, writing now

CHORUS:

MEG CHRISTIAN AND HOLLY NEAR

Radical
Feminism

the woman whose head is on fire

the woman whose head is on fire
the woman with a noisy voice
the woman with too many fingers
the woman who never smiled once in her life
the woman with a boney body
the woman with moles all over her

the woman who cut off her breast
the woman with a large bobbing head
the woman with one glass eye
the woman with broad shoulders
the woman with callused elbows
the woman with a sunken chest
the woman who is part giraffe

the woman with five gold teeth
the woman who looks straight ahead
the woman with enormous knees
the woman who can lick her own clitoris
the woman who screams on the trumpet
the woman whose toes grew together
the woman who says I am what I am

the woman with rice under her skin
the woman who owns a machete
the woman who plants potatoes
the woman who murders the kangaroo
the woman who stuffs clothing into a sack
the woman who makes a great racket
the woman who fixes machines
the woman whose chin is sticking out
the woman who says I will be

the woman who carries laundry on her head
the woman who is part horse
the woman who asks so many questions
the woman who cut somebody's throat

the woman who gathers peaches
the woman who carries jars on her head
the woman who howls
the woman whose nose is broken
the woman who constructs buildings

the woman who has fits on the floor
the woman who makes rain happen
the woman who refuses to menstruate

the woman who sets broken bones
the woman who sleeps out on the street
the woman who plays the drum

the woman who is part grasshopper
the woman who herds cattle
the woman whose will is unbending
the woman who hates kittens

the woman who escaped from the jailhouse
the woman who is walking across the desert
the woman who buries the dead
the woman who taught herself writing
the woman who skins rabbits
the woman who believes her own word
the woman who chews bearskin
the woman who eats cocaine
the woman who thinks about everything

the woman who has the tattoo of a bird
the woman who puts things together
the woman who squats on her haunches
the woman whose children are all different colors

singing   i am the will of the woman
                   the woman
                   my will is unbending

when She-Who-moves-the-earth will turn over
when She Who moves, the earth will turn over.

JUDY GRAHN

From the series "She Who," in Judy Grahn, *The Work of a Common Woman*
(Trumansberg, N.Y.: Crossing Press, 1980). Originally published in Judy Grahn,
She Who: A Graphic Book of Poems (Oakland, Calif.: Diana Press, 1977).
Copyright © 1977 by Judy Grahn. Used with permission.

A Radical Feminist Perspective

Lib Hutchison

Using the concept of patriarchy as a primary analytic mechanism, the author questions the most basic structures of society that we tend to regard as inevitable and immutable. Her practice, which is designed to foster individual empowerment and institutional change, is necessarily generalist in nature. In describing this practice, she discusses how she uses consciousness-raising techniques and diversity as an organizing principle, builds coalitions, and promotes collaborative forms of leadership. She also suggests implications of the feminist perspective for teaching social work practice and for the structure of social work education. ——Editor's Note

I am a feminist in process and expect always to be a feminist in process. I am confident that future life experience will reshape the perspective expressed in this article. Some aspects of my current understanding will be validated, others will be expanded, some will become intensified, some will be modified, and a few probably will be discarded. When I learn of another social worker's practice theories, I am curious about the pathways that person took to the current theoretical perspective—those events and experiences that contributed to the social worker's uniqueness. So, I would like to begin by sharing some of my pathways with you.

MY BACKGROUND

I was born 38 years ago in rural Tennessee and moved from a farm to a small town when I was 9 years old. Among the early significant influences in my life were the numerous biographies of adventurous women that I read while sitting in a three-room country schoolhouse in Yankeetown, Tennessee. A prominent role model was my grandmother, the wife of a Presbyterian missionary who had been assigned to develop a parish in rural Tennessee. On becoming a widow in her fifties, my grandmother picked up much of her husband's religious and community development work and worked actively,

Lib Hutchison, MSW, director of the undergraduate social work program at Elms College, Chicopee, Massachusetts, is a social work educator with a practice background primarily in rural areas. She has been active in the women's movement for many years, often working on issues and problems faced by middle-aged caregivers.

without pay, until her death at age 84. I attended elementary school in the 1950s and high school in the early 1960s, influenced little by the budding civil rights movement or anything else that was political.

After graduation from high school, I attended a small Presbyterian college in East Tennessee, being the only female in my high school class to go "away to school." My friends thought that I was adventurous to journey three hours from home to attend college. While in college, I became interested in and peripherally involved in the civil rights movement. In my sophomore year, I was stimulated by the feminist teacher of a course on social problems to read *The Feminine Mystique* by Betty Friedan. This book was my introduction to ideas of sexism, and I felt the world opening up. The same teacher later served as an adviser for my senior thesis on "Women and Work." After graduating from college, I went to the George Warren Brown School of Social Work at Washington University, St. Louis, Missouri. Washington University was actually my second choice of graduate schools; I went there after receiving a lengthy rejection letter from Columbia University, which stated that I was academically qualified but that my life experiences in the rural South had not prepared me for life in New York City or for study at Columbia University. This letter was the first time that I was conscious of being an object of prejudice.

While in graduate school, I became involved in the civil rights movement but had no serious involvement in feminist thinking or activity. This lack of involvement seemed to have been true of many other young women in the late 1960s. On leaving graduate school, I worked for three years as a medical social worker in a large teaching hospital. There I learned that it is one thing to hold feminist views intellectually and another thing to "hang tough" in a classist, racist, and sexist institution. My socialization as a "good southern girl" did not teach the assertiveness skills that were essential for such a setting. I was mentally tough but weak in social skills. I felt oppressed daily and came to feel that in my work with clients I was often the oppressor as well—even though my supervisor (and role model) was a strongly assertive and empowering woman.

I retreated into motherhood, or so I thought. Like many middle-class women of my age group, in the recesses of my mind I held the notion that "if this liberation stuff does not work out (or becomes too hard), I'll have babies." I probably assumed that I would then be taken care of. So, I became a mother and then I really had my consciousness raised. I spent five difficult years getting in touch with my anger at the definitions my culture had given me and at myself for accepting them without a greater struggle. I bonded with other young mothers and worked with other local feminists to develop a feminist day care center and to create educational alternatives for educationally deprived young women. At age 32, I reentered the world of paid social work with a heady and growing sense of empowerment and a firm belief that I did not have to be either oppressed or an oppressor. Maintaining that belief has been a struggle because patriarchy goes deep, but I continue to work at it, with pain and with hope.

INFLUENCE OF FEMINISM ON MY PRACTICE

My difficult struggle to get in touch with my power and the many things that I learned from bonding with other women allowed me to begin to integrate my cognitive, physical, social, emotional, spiritual, and political selves. From then on, I could no longer practice a social work that did not include an integrated approach. Now I am a generalist social worker. I cannot ignore individual pain, but I feel a strong commitment to look for systemic causes and to work for institutional change as well as to empower individuals. I believe that good helping flows from *needs*—not from agency mandates or pet theories and skills.

My experience with empowering networks influenced me to develop a demonstration project for the Administration on Aging to "Identify and Enhance the Natural Support Systems for Rural Elders." In this work, I focused especially on helping middle-aged caregivers of impaired elderly people to develop support networks and to use them for advocacy. Now I teach social work to undergraduate students at a Roman Catholic women's college in New England. My experiences with growing and becoming led me to seek and accept such a position. Because in our society and our profession, progress in reassessing sex-role socialization has been slow, I want to help empower other women to know themselves, their needs, and their potential, as well as the social systems in which they operate. I also believe that the social work profession can be an empowering profession and I want to influence future social workers to see it that way.

Practice Principles that Flow from my Feminism

Social work relationships. Egalitarianism is the most just and realistic form of relationship. Mutuality and reciprocity are good guidelines for the social worker–client relationship. We should, at all times, remain professionally humble. I have spent too many years undoing the work of former generations of social workers who acted on professional wisdom to believe that I have all the answers. We must often give up the "expert" status and learn to derive satisfaction from watching others get in touch with their "expertise." After several years of observation, I am convinced that innovation begins at the grass-roots level—not at the "establishment" professional level. As professionals, our job should be to remain close to grass-roots efforts, to respond to and legitimate them when appropriate. We should support networking, support, and self-help groups. Collaborative forms of leadership can and do work. Coalition building is an effective planning and organizing tool—one that feminist practitioners can use to enable new, politically effective relationships among diverse groups.

Social work roles. Social work is a science and an art, and neither sex can be excused from either side of the duality. All social workers, male and female, should be competent and effective in the nurturing roles of enabler and facilitator and the more assertive roles of advocate and organizer. To distribute or emphasize these roles according to sex, as has often been the practice in social work, legitimates and perpetuates sexist oppression.

Social work assessment. Most social workers would agree that life is too complex for one-dimensional assessment and planning. Yet too few of us regularly reflect the complexities of the person-in-environment transactions in assessment and planning activities. There is no place in social work for "blaming the victims," whether the victims are women or other devalued people. Although this statement seems obvious, I believe that the social work assessment process regularly includes blaming-the-victims thinking. Recently, I heard a mental health worker describe a homeless woman—a mother of three small children—as "unmotivated" because the woman had not found shelter for her family. In reality, a housing specialist had been working with this woman for three months to find housing but had not been successful because of the severe housing shortage for low-income families in that city. A common example of blaming the victim occurs when social workers describe their clients as hostile and resistant when the client's behavior often is an appropriate response to the social worker's method and style of initiating services.

Process and task. Both process and task are important. Any means of assisting clients, communities, or agencies to achieve goals should safeguard the dignity and self-esteem of the involved parties. Qualitative as well as quantitative research methods are needed to advance our knowledge base, and process as well as outcome evaluation helps us to evaluate the effectiveness of our work.

Structure of social work services. The current specialized structures for delivering social services militate against services based on need and against preventive programs directed toward institutional change. We must immediately address this issue in the profession to provide a service structure that is consonant with and supportive of our wholistic and needs-based practice philosophy.

Mobilizing for change. Multidimensional thinking demands that feminists not allow the feminist movement to become a middle-class movement but suggests that we must bond with groups who are struggling with such issues as classism and racism. Diversity is stimulating; we should respect and encourage diverse views of feminism but maintain enough focus to become a powerful force for change. Basic change is essential. We cannot be satisfied with illusions of progress, nor should middle-class women be content to satisfy their drive for success at the expense of other women. To create new opportunities for women without changing the *structure* of opportunity will merely set women against women, women against people of color, and women against working-class men. This is not a feminist solution to sexism.

I am convinced that the feminist answer for women in social work is not to become just like traditional men or to continue to allow some worthwhile traditional feminine traits to be devalued in the profession. Healing wounds is different work from administering programs, but it is no less important. Men and women can do both kinds of work. Women's tendency to solve ethical dilemmas based on human connectedness could create more humane and more effective service institutions.[1] We should not be so quick to assume that the power-and-control methods of men at the top are the only methods for establishing and maintaining leadership positions. Miller's words can guide us in our search to integrate our need for affiliation and for achievement:

> Women are quite validly seeking something more complete than autonomy as it is defined by men, a fuller not lesser ability to encompass relationships to others, simultaneously with the fullest development of oneself.[2]

REFERENCES

1. Carol Gilligan, *In a Different Voice* (Cambridge, Mass.: Harvard University Press, 1982).

2. Jean Baker Miller, *Toward a New Psychology of Women* (Boston: Beacon Press, 1976), pp. 94–95.

I LIKE TO THINK OF HARRIET TUBMAN

I like to think of Harriet Tubman.
Harriet Tubman who carried a revolver,
who had a scar on her head from a rock thrown
by a slave-master (because she
talked back), and who
had a ransom on her head
of thousands of dollars and who
was never caught, and who
had no use for the law
when the law was wrong,
who defied the law. I like
to think of her.
I like to think of her especially
when I think of the problem of
feeding children.

The legal answer
to the problem of feeding children
is ten free lunches every month,
being equal, in the child's real life,
to eating lunch every other day.
Monday but not Tuesday.
I like to think of the President
eating lunch Monday, but not
Tuesday.
And when I think of the President
and the law, and the problem of
feeding children, I like to
think of Harriet Tubman
and her revolver.

And then sometimes
I think of the President
and other men,
men who practice the law,
who revere the law,
who make the law,
who enforce the law,
who live behind
and operate through
and feed themselves
at the expense of
serving children
because of the law.

Men who sit in paneled offices
and think about vacations
and tell women
whose care it is

to feed children
not to be hysterical
not to be hysterical as in the word
hysterikos, the greek for
womb suffering,
not to suffer in their
wombs,
not to care,
not to bother the men
because they want to think
of other things
and do not want
to take the women seriously.
I want them
to take women seriously.

I want them to think about Harriet Tubman,
and remember,
remember she was beat by a white man
and she lived
and she lived to redress her grievances,
and she lived in swamps
and wore the clothes of a man
bringing hundreds of fugitives from
slavery, and was never caught,
and led an army,
and won a battle,
and defied the laws
because the laws were wrong. I want men
to take us seriously.
I am tired of wanting them to think
about right and wrong.
I want them to fear.

I want them to feel fear now
as I have felt suffering in the womb, and
I want them
to know
that there is always a time
there is always a time to make right
what is wrong,
there is always a time
for retribution
and that time
is beginning.

SUSAN GRIFFIN

Socialist
Feminism

THE RECEPTIONIST IS BY DEFINITION

her personal life has very little to do with
this grim determination. telephone lines constrict
her arms and legs.
    1. the receptionist is by definition
        always interruptable.

she cut two people off today in one punch
of the button. the pencil is hooked with
string to the phone so no one can walk off
        with her.

'will you hold please? I'll see if he's in.'
(are you in?)
'I'm sorry, sir, he's out.'
    2. the receptionist is by definition
        underpaid to lie.

remember the receptionist with the lovely
smile, with the green eyes, the cropped
hair, big feet, small knees, with the
wrinkled hands, the large breasts, with
the husky voice, the strong chin?
    she takes her breaks
in the washroom, grimacing, waving her fists
at the blurred reflection of her dress.

KAREN BRODINE

From *Workweek: Poems by Karen Brodine* (Berkeley, Calif.: Kelsey Street Press, 1977).
Copyright © 1976 by Karen Brodine. Reprinted by permission of the author.

A Socialist
Feminist Perspective

K. C. Wagner

This article is a case study of a feminist organization: of its direct service, educational, and organizing work with and on behalf of women who experience sexual harrassment on the job and how its workers attempted to deal with the "contradictions of working and living in a capitalist system." The article describes the process of a small women's organization operating on a shoestring budget and volunteer efforts that became bureaucratized and professionalized, the ensuing disempowerment and unwitting collusion of the workers who "internalized the contradictions of policy and practice," their confrontation of these contradictions, and their successful struggle to reclaim their vision and the social change mission of the organization. ——Editor's Note

Working Women's Institute began in 1975 in Ithaca, New York, with a community "Speak Out" that featured the struggle of a single working mother, who was employed at the local university, against unwanted and uninvited sexual attentions. This event drew a cross section of working women from the university and the community. It labeled a common work-related experience that, until that time, had been shrouded in silence and reflected the unequal power position that women assumed on the job. At the Speak Out, a major commitment was made to work toward the empowerment of working women and especially to combat sexual harassment on the job. This local organizing effort touched a national nerve, and the organization started to disseminate its research and other information on rights and workplace strategies across the country. Originally, there were two program components—the organizing arm called Working Women United and the nonprofit educational arm called Working Women United Institute. The latter component had a board of directors and a staff, which was formed along hierarchical lines.

TRANSITION TO NEW YORK

When the organization moved to New York City in 1977, it retained the name, functions, and hierarchical structure of Working Women United Institute. The

K. C. Wagner, MSW, is Program Director, Working Women's Institute, and an activist in New York City. She organizes groups and coalitions to expose and end sexual harassment and gender bias in the workplace and the many forms of violence against undocumented women aliens.

rationale was that it was the only way to be "taken seriously" and to "look legitimate" to the foundation world. However, the staff still operated on a volunteer basis and a shoestring budget; everyone did everything, from proposal writing to counseling. Hence, contrary to how it was described on paper, the organization was still small, horizontally structured, working out of a basement of a church, and operating much like a workers' collective.

Foundation money came in slowly at first (enough to hire part-time staff) and then more rapidly (enough to to hire full-time and support staff). The organization developed in two ways. First, the division of labor became more defined; second, decision making increasingly reflected hierarchical positions, and it moved from consensus to executive-level decision making. The rationale was, "We don't have the luxury of time to discuss things, we have to prove ourselves now." People reluctantly let go of their fantasies but turned to the "corporate model" as the only way to become successful. At the time, no one realized how ironic this decision would be.

What were some everyday implications of this change in structure and decision making? The first reaction was relief because the line staff members finally were able to focus on program areas and were not distracted by other needs of the overall organization. However, the problem with this narrowed focus was that administrative tasks or executive privileges, such as budgetary information, decisions about programs, and proposal writing, also became increasingly centralized. Lines of accountability were drawn from the top down, and staff was kept separate by one-to-one meetings and supervision. Assignments that involved the media, public appearances, or travel were guarded. Consequently, tensions mounted.

CONTRADICTIONS

Despite the stated goal of the organization to empower working women and challenge the inequities they face as women and as workers, the internal structure was in direct opposition to it. Rather, the internal structure created oppressive working conditions that disempowered, demoralized, and depressed a staff of bright, assertive, creative progressive women, who would have been outraged and indignant if they had heard of such a situation happening to another working woman!

Why did it happen? How could it happen? We spent the next 1½ years discovering the contradictions and personal inconsistencies that contributed to a workplace that became less like a feminist organization and more like a mini corporation. Then we developed an organizing strategy that eventually led to a major restructuring of the organization.

Our story began like any classic story of organizing—by talking to each other. We discovered that the issues we internalized as personal were structural. We worried about the security of our jobs and were afraid of disrupting the organization and sacrificing the work of the organization. Our silence was contributing to the status quo. Once we broke down this isolation, we knew that our combined experience and contacts would offer some solutions. Subcommittees were formed to research resources, talk to other groups, and draw from materials on nontraditional organizations.[1] We even met with an organizational consultant. We found that we were struggling with the following major contradictions in our effort to create an organization that reflected and supported our feminist values and commitments: hierarchy versus equalized power, one-way versus group accountability, centralized versus decentralized control of information, "top down" versus group decision making, product versus process, adversarial versus reciprocal working relationships, and an individual versus collective orientation.

In fall 1981, we started operating as an organization that attempted to incorporate the political principles of its staff. Despite some minor changes in staff, we retained a hierarchical structure. However, until August 1983, we successfully incorporated some of the principles of feminist management, including cooperative and democratic styles of administration, a rotating grievance committee, a salary policy based on an average wage with adjustments for seniority and the quality of one's work, reconceptualized notions of power (which acknowledged times when it is hard to give it up), the value of talk as well as action, a criticism–self-criticism exercise after each meeting, and a more equitable redistribution of the "perks" attached to job status, to name a few. Our process was clearly dialectical, although the issues were not always apparent.

However, we could not make magic, and in July 1983, we made the collective decision to cut staff by August 1983 because of the loss of foundation support and the conservative backlash against priorities, programs, and services to women. It was a sad but realistic decision; we wanted to preserve our energies, mental health, and accomplishments. We then spent the next month ending services we could no longer provide, training other groups to take over our counseling program, and rewriting our materials for public use.

We believed the only way to go through this painful process was to do it together. In January 1984, four staff members remained on a part-time basis to transfer our remaining resources to other organizations and to provide limited education, technical assistance, and training to the public and private sectors on a fee-for-service and volunteer basis. One staff member wrote a proposal for a book, based on her research at the institute. All of us found some other type of part-time work. Two former staff members, who started full-time jobs in related fields, use the skills they perfected or acquired at the institute. Despite our personal losses, we felt satisfied with the way we ended or transferred our work. Most important, we preserved and even strengthened our personal relationships in doing so. Perhaps a time will come when we can reemerge.

EPILOGUE

In October 1984, almost a year after the Institute on Feminist Practice, the Working Women's Institute was on its way back! Among the reasons was a recent contract to conduct a survey of training needs in relation to sexual harassment for a major public sector employer. This retransformation into a viable organization was due to many factors. First, streamlining our programs helped to reduce the drain on scarce resources and gave us maximum flexibility. Second, the ability of the staff to obtain and juggle part-time jobs was critical to the survival of the organization, although frustrating. Third, the efforts over the years to build a healthy organization— internally and with the board—paid off. And fourth, four women's organizations—the Center for Women in Government, in Albany; New York Women Against Rape, and Women's Counseling, in New York City; and the Women's Rights Law Reporter of Rutgers Law School, Newark, New Jersey— provided support and were willing to incorporate the services or programs we were unable to provide.

During the year of transformation and reemergence, we continued to provide ongoing training and support for the volunteers and staffs of those organizations that agreed to meet the direct service needs of the women with whom we had worked. Gradually, new roles began to crystalize for us, emerging from and stimulated by at least two forces: the opportunity to "market" our expertise to employers and our feminist commitment to continue to address the issue of sexual harassment in a manner that reflected our values. We knew that these two forces were potentially oppositional and raised a new set of contradictions for us.

The "marketing" opportunities, ironically, resulted in large measure from our grass-roots organizing efforts over the years to *name* sexual harassment for what it was—a form of violence against women—and to create a consensus that it must and would stop. We had demanded that employers act, irrespective of their politics, to identify and end sexual harassment in their workplaces. Now at least one large employer had said, in effect, "show us that it exists and, if it does, show us what to do about it." Our analysis of the dynamics of sexual harassment was such that we believed in the need to continue to agitate and organize at the community level. How could we do this while relying for our income on employers, both public and private, against whom we were pressing demands? Could we do this and not "sell out"?

During this past year, we have been grappling with that question. We adopted and refined the new roles created by the contract with the public sector employer and have obtained contracts with other employers, both public and private. We focused on research and evaluation, consultation and technical assistance, and education and training. We have enlarged our purview to include all areas of gender bias in the workplace. And we have adopted a frankly entrepreneurial strategy to "sell" this package of services to employers.

To do so while holding firmly to our political analysis and commitments, we are attending carefully to several critical areas, informed by our feminism. For example, we watch our language. We use nonthreatening language in our written materials and presentations. We rewrote our mission statement to qualify for some types of funding. We consciously seek and build on areas of agreement with employers and managers and then push the issue of sexual harassment from a political perspective. We will not compromise that perspective, so we know that some employers will not hire us. We continue to root ourselves in the community and among workers. We have worked with shop stewards and the rank and file, training women to recognize, confront, and stop sexual harassment. We have served as expert witnesses for the plaintiff in several cases and consult with the attorneys of victims of sexual harassment. Building on our analysis, we have participated actively with other groups concerned with sexual harassment and other forms of violence against an extremely vulnerable group: undocumented women workers from the Asian, Pacific Island, and Carribean communities. This coalition approach, grounded in our feminist strategy, has attracted the interest of foundations.

In sum, through a combined funding strategy of earned income and foundation funding, the Working Women's Institute has been able to survive. Although our programs and roles have changed, we have been able to ensure that direct service needs continue to be met through sister organizations who share our analysis and commitments. Our organizational transformation, particularly the incorporation of entrepreneurial and employer-sponsored funding strategies, has raised a new set of contradictions and challenges to our feminist practice. But our refusal to compromise, combined with our insistence on holding firm to feminist analysis and process, to engage in criticism/self-criticism, to stay rooted in the struggles and experiences of women workers, and to build community-based coalitions have preserved our character as a progressive feminist organization. We are proceeding with caution and with courage.

REFERENCES

1. Karen Brandow, Jim McDonnell, and Vocations for Social Change, *No Bosses Here!* (2d ed.; Boston: Alyson Publications, 1981); Virginia Coover et al., *Resource Manual for a Living Revolution* (Philadelphia: New Society Press, 1977); Nancy Hooyman and Cheryl Ellsworth, "Toward A Feminist Adminsitrative Style," paper presented at the First NASW National Conference on Women in Social Work, Washington, D.C., September 1980; Mel Morgenbesser et al., "The Evolution of Three Alternative Social Service Agencies," *Catalyst*, 11 (1981), pp. 77–83; Sheila Rowbotham, Lynne Segal, and Hilary Wainwright, *Beyond the Fragments: Feminism and the Making of Socialism* (Boston: Alyson Publications, 1981); Rowbotham, *Man's World, Women's Consciousness* (New York: Penguin Books, 1973); and Steve Burghardt, *The Other Side of Organizing* (Cambridge, Mass.: Schenkman Publishing Co., 1982).

EMMA

This summer I dreamed that Emma Goldman
came to a theatre workshop.
She was quite hepped up about
what was happening at fifth avenue and fiftieth street
for instance
across from the cathedral and down the street from Bergdorf's.
She wanted to make certain that we were politically aware
of the implications of our existence.
So she marched out into the center of our workspace
wearing a long dark cape
high boots and white petticoats that
frothed at the bottom of her heavy skirt
as she kicked the stage clear of crates and claptrap
and adjusted her glasses with a quick push of an index finger.

Before anyone could put her through the questioner
she snapped
"You there: climb the walls
You there: beat your breast
You there: prostrate yourself before atlas holding up
the world right smack in the middle of rockefeller center
at fifth avenue and fiftieth street.

And don't tell me that if I want to lecture the audience
I should write a political tract
because what you have here is character and situation.

You there: repeat the word collectivity fast
until it sounds like the hoofbeats of a horse running wild
with the news that we are all
up against the wall of economic oppression.
Because what you have here is character and situation
and the potential for women who are moving together
to move away from just carving out for themselves
a bigger piece of the capitalist pie."

What becomes a legend most?
Her visions.
Her life's work.
Her hard realities.

And I dreamed that the world's womanline rose up
to occupy rockefeller center
which came to be known as the new york based world wide

women's center for international peace and equal justice
and clean air and water
and the very fish in the sea
leaped up and splashed the ozone layer with their joy
because finally
mere anarchy was loosed upon the land.

Needless to say, atlas never got it up again.

CLARE COSS

the questioner—a theater research form used to elicit thematic material.

Women of Color

TO THE 'MAJORITY' FROM A 'MINORITY'

i did not come by faith.
how i came is not your business
but if you must know,
i came by any means i could and
any means necessary,
i came by bus
by mastercharge
by crying and carrying on.
i came by leaning on my Momma who leaned on the
Lord who leaned on Southern Comfort.
i came
in crowds
in secret codes
in raging and wrath sometimes i came,
barely.   and alone.
now,
it is not your business,
how i came and i can't stand
nosey people but
this is your business.

i am not going back.
so here i am.
but what
i am, really,
ain't your business.

Doris Davenport

From Eat Thunder and Drink Rain (published by the author, 1982). Copyright © 1979 by Doris Davenport. First appeared in *Feminary,* Vol. II (1981). Reprinted by permission of the author.

YELLOW WOMAN SPEAKS

Shadow become real; follower become leader;
    mouse turned sorcerer—

In a red sky, a darker beast lies waiting,
    her teeth, once hidden, now unsheathed swords.

Yellow woman, a revolutionary speaks:

"They have mutilated our genitals, but I will
    restore them;
I will render our shames and praise them,
Our beauties, our mothers:
Those young Chinese whores on display in barracoons;
the domestics in soiled aprons;
the miners, loggers, railroad workers
    holed up in Truckee in winters.
                I will create armies of their descendents.

And I will expose the lies and ridicule
the impotence of those who have called us
    chink
    yellow-livered
    slanted cunts
    exotic
in order to abuse and exploit us.
              And I will destroy them."

Abrasive teacher, incisive comedian,
Painted Lady, dark domestic—
Sweep minds' attics; burnish our senses;
keep house, make love, wreak vengeance.

MERLE WOO

WOMANIST

Womanist:

1. From womanish (Opp. of "girlish," i.e., frivolous, irresponsible, not serious.) A black feminist or feminist of color. From the black folk expression of mothers to female children, "You acting womanish," i.e., like a woman. Usually referring to outrageous, audacious, courageous or willful behavior. Wanting to know more and in greater depth than is considered "good" for one. Interested in grown-up doings. Acting grown up. Being grown up. Interchangeable with another black folk expression: "You trying to be grown." Responsible. In charge. Serious.

2. Also: A woman who loves other women, sexually and/or nonsexually. Appreciates and prefers women's culture, women's emotional flexibility (values tears as natural counterbalance of laughter), and women's strength. Sometimes loves individual men, sexually and/or nonsexually. Committed to survival and wholeness of entire people, male and female. Not a separatist, except periodically, for health. Traditionally universalist, as in: "Mama, why are we brown, pink, and yellow, and our cousins are white, beige, and black?" Ans: "Well, you know the colored race is just like a flower garden, with every color flower represented." Traditionally capable, as in: "Mama, I'm walking to Canada and I'm taking you and a bunch of other slaves with me." Reply: "It wouldn't be the first time."

3. Loves music. Loves dance. Loves the moon. Loves the Spirit. Loves love and food and roundness. Loves struggle. Loves the Folk. Loves herself. Regardless.

4. Womanist is to feminist as purple to lavender.

ALICE WALKER

Women of Color and Feminist Practice

Members of SOURCE,
Black Women Therapists' Collective:
Zoleka Adams-Sawyer
Martha Adams-Sullivan
Robyn Brown-Manning
Andaye C. DeLaCruz
Carmen Gaines

Members of SOURCE: The Black Women Therapists' Collective describe their work and its underlying assumptions, a central one being that the oppression of women cannot be addressed without addressing the conditions of color, class, and sexual orientation. For them, the first concern must be the implications of color: black women helping black women is a survival imperative. A unilateral feminist ideology that emerges from the experience of white women alone cannot cross racial and class barriers. The work of SOURCE is directed to the amelioration of the effects of all forms of oppression in the lives of individuals and families. To accomplish this goal, members of SOURCE use a wide variety of techniques, including healing processes rooted in African culture. Other dimensions of their work are directed at changing social and political systems that are oppressive and developing those which are liberating. This article is a collective effort by the members of SOURCE. Formed by graduates of the Hunter College School of Social Work in New York City in response to a felt need to create a practice which "talked about us as black women," the collective is active in the greater New York area. ——Editor's Note

Note: The editors and members of SOURCE agree that no one group can represent and speak for all women of color. As with the other presenters, the members of SOURCE were asked to illustrate a certain perspective, not to represent it. As the authors point out, for us to fail to acknowledge and work with the uniqueness of each individual and cultural group is inherently oppressive.

WHO WE ARE

SOURCE: The Black Women Therapists' Collective was cofounded in October 1978 by 12 graduates of the Hunter College School of Social Work in New York City. As a black professional resource group, our purpose is to provide alternative perspectives in healing services and to introduce techniques and skills so that individuals can cope creatively with the effects of social and political pressures on their lives.

A clear understanding of how and why SOURCE got together is critical for the purpose of this article. In October 1978, we had been out of school a little over two years. We were working in a variety of settings: child welfare agencies, mental health agencies, hospitals, and alcohol treatment programs, as well as in private practice. Conversations between the members at various times revealed a disturbing situation; something was *not* happening for us in the field. Regardless of the agency or setting in which we were working, we were feeling isolated and alienated. Traditional methods of intervention were not comfortable to use, nor were they working with our clients. Our host agencies were not enthusiastic, much less supportive, of our attempts to use more innovative techniques. The overwhelming nature of the forces of racism, sexism, and classism that are inherent in social work practice were (and still are) too much for any one of us to deal with alone and still be expected to function.

Case in point: It is not an uncommon experience for black professionals to be asked to speak on an issue that is race related. Why were we not approached to present a socialist perspective, a radical perspective, or one of the other orientations to practice that were being presented at the institute? Why are black women, or women of color, presented as a "tendency" in feminism?

Feminist language often contains clear descriptive divisions. There are "feminists" and there are "black feminists"; there are "women" and there are "women of color." That it is understood that the words "feminist" and "women" standing alone are not inclusive of all women, regardless of ethnicity, is racism in full operation. For the women of SOURCE, it is this very racism, which cuts across issues of class and sex, that causes us to choose to struggle through our concerns with other black women. Furthermore, SOURCE came together as a black women therapists' group clearly in response to the issue that feminists, particularly feminist psychotherapists in their practices, were not dealing with the subject of racism as a priority, if they were dealing with it at all.

Thus SOURCE was born, not necessarily out of some grandiose notion that we were going to right all the wrongs and injustices of the world, but out of our need to survive. SOURCE was born from the recognition that, as black women professionals working in a society in which we were triply oppressed, and in which every institution of that society was actively operating to keep us that way, we had better turn to each other if we were to maintain any semblance of health—any semblance of self.

A COLLECTIVE

That we came together as black women therapists was a conscious decision. However, SOURCE's operational style, in itself, is not unique; it merely illustrates how black people traditionally and historically have functioned in a collective manner. Our choice of the word "collective" is important to us. It is the spirit of the collective that determines and guides our practice and is our connection to each other, our people, and our sense of collective responsibility in changing the conditions that are toxic to our well-being.

As black women we recognize and are proud of our coming from a historical tradition of women helping women. Were it not for the strength of our sisterhood, which began with village life in Africa and continued throughout our dispersal, through slavery and all the way to the alienation and isolation we feel in the contemporary world (even in human service agencies), we know that we could not have survived. We know that our notion of extended family is much present in our world. We are a family connected by kinship, hardship, blood lines, shared experience, or struggle.

The word "collective" states how we work. We are a nonhierarchial organization which believes that each person's contribution is of equal value and that the distribution of work and decisions to be made are shared by all. Hence, we are all leaders; we are all followers. However, we are, at the same time, mindful of the individual freedom that each of us has, and we treasure and support each other's right to disagree. We confront and struggle with the contradictions that are part of life in this society, both within and outside ourselves.

We know and have experienced the superior power of the collective as a unit and its ability to empower and direct individual energies. We have come together to do seminars, workshops, and political work and to write. But each of us has "strangely" noted that SOURCE has "sourced" each of us moving up and out into the world to produce. SOURCE knows that without the support and caring of each other, life would not be the same. We know that our collective strength is more than any of us individually could ever have.

We know that there is a fine or nondistinct line between the personal, the clinical, and the political. One's practice is determined by one's values and one's view of the world. SOURCE, as a collective of women of African descent, knows clearly that change comes from individuals who organized together for a common goal. We are committed to offering the healing of ourselves, our people, and society as it is presently organized through our practice and our political work.

MISCONCEPTIONS ABOUT BLACK WOMEN

Often, because of national chauvinism, class perspective, racism, and sexism, we in SOURCE have encountered a series of misconceptions about black women and black women's groups. First, black women's groups often are seen as hierarchical organizations of women—in the traditional Western, male, class-oriented organizational style—in which one person is considered the leader or trend setter and the others are followers, and the strength of collective work is ignored. Other misconceptions also exist. For example, usually it is thought that the term "black women" is synonymous with Afro-American women from the United States. Assumptions are then made about a cultural tradition based only on the experience of black women in that particular social reality. Another misconception we have encountered as a progressive black women therapists' group is that we would view sexism as the primary oppression experienced by black women. Both these assumptions are incorrect with respect to SOURCE.

Our use of the term "black women" refers to all women of African descent—not only those from all walks of life in the United States, but those from Central and Latin America, the Caribbean, Africa, and the world over. As a collective that is part of the Third World women's community in particular and the women's community in general, we support the progressive struggle of all our sisters. Yet we in SOURCE recognize the double-edged sword that imperialism has wielded against the lives of both men and women of color. African peoples, women included, have been dispersed to every corner of the world, making us diverse in language, cultures, customs, and psychological makeup. We are not homogeneous. The concerns of black women, like those of the men and children of our national groups, are molded by our various cultures and social realities.

At the same time, although racism has taken on particular forms in different regions of the world, the reality and treatment of black women and women of color in general, have been similar. Racism has, for the most part, placed us in the lower strata of any society in which we are found. Racism binds women of color to a heritage of triple oppression—work by force and not by choice, constant struggle, and resistance. As women of color, our oppression as women, be we lesbian or heterosexual, single or married, does not take precedence over and cannot be treated without simultaneously addressing our social conditions in relation to our color and our class. The term "black women" also implies adherence to particular social norms that reflect values and customs of family life, child rearing, child care, work, religion, and support systems that are rooted in African culture and traditions. These social norms often are in contradiction with the values of Western society, theories, and practices.

Wherever the institution of racism has existed, the black woman has been characterized as the antithesis of what is considered sacred or strong in womanhood. We are characterized as workhorses, breeders, pillars of strength, passive about women's issues, and antifeminist, all in one breath. Ironically, the same women's movement that emulates our image denies our struggles. It denies the history of its own origins and fails to address our concerns.

In short, we have found that the concept of a unilateral feminine experience and ideology—one that crosses the barriers of race, class, and sexual preference—is a myth. Women are made different and arrive at womanhood with different concerns by virtue of our different social realities. A white middle-class single-parent household, heterosexual or lesbian, does not function with the same economic stress as a working-class single-parent household, lesbian or heterosexual, black or white.

Although we support struggles against the oppression of women in relation to sexual preference and against chauvinism, patriarchy, and paternalism, we find that clinical-political treatment of these issues cannot be done in a vacuum. There is a need for culturally relevant clinical intervention that takes into consideration race and class.

We are clear, however, that the changes that need to occur in individual life will not take place without a total change in the structure of this society. But we see ourselves and our work as "in process" toward those changes in life.

GOALS AND ACTIVITIES

SOURCE is concerned with the delivery of high-quality healing services that are free of class bias, racial prejudice, and sexual stereotypes. Our purpose is to learn, rediscover, and introduce techniques and skills for creatively coping with life. Our goals are as follows:

■ To provide healing processes that will help individuals let go of emotional, physical, and spiritual toxins.

■ To offer techniques and skills that will assist in positively changing feelings, attitudes, and behavior.

■ To provide a therapeutic process that will give support and nurturance.

■ To help individuals regain the ability to make decisions and respond to self, situations, and environment.

■ To heighten awareness of the manifestations and effects of oppression on life.

Our members work in a variety of fields—day care, alcoholism, data processing, child guidance, geriatrics, and education—and in various ways. We utilize techniques and therapies that are as diverse as we are. Astrology, political activism, Gestalt techniques, analytically oriented individual and group techniques, psychic healing, policy and planning, family therapy and education, to name a few. We endorse any process that nonoppressively facilitates our goals. So, how are we different from any other group with similarly stated goals? More important, how are we, as diverse group members, alike?

We are alike in that we hold some basic views about the nature of humankind, our place in the universe, the nature of this society, and the lack of complementarity of these factors. We believe that the individual is a product of her cultural base, political and economic conditions, community, and family. We believe that an individual comes to the world with some innate characteristics that are connected to the historical, cultural, economic, and political conditions of the group into which she is born. Thus, the individual embodies the sum total of our existence as well as being "a new beginning." We understand that all things in the universe are interdependent. We are spiritual beings who are not separate from our environments.

We do not, as some would glibly say, "take culture into account." Rather, we recognize that human behavior is a product of culture and culture is a product of human behavior. As Horton and Hunt noted, culture defines situations, attitudes, values, goals, and behavioral patterns and gives "answers for the imponderables of life."[1] It is within one's culture that one lives and dreams, defines the world, and shapes the theories that govern norms for reality, behavior, and health.

Because the concept of health is culturally determined, we, like Pasteur and Tolson, draw a sharp distinction between "health" and "normality."[2] To use the individual as an example, we define as "healthy" a state of well-being in which an individual can act in the environment with integrity, spontaneity, and an integrated mind, body, emotion, and spirit.

To be "normal," on the other hand, requires the control or regulation of individuals to fulfill successfully a role (or several roles) in a group or society. To be "normal" in this racist, sexist, and elitist society, which stresses individualism, "rationality," and separation of the "sacred and profane" and which values the assimilation of peoples and the accommodation of cultures, means to be at odds with our culture, values, norms, traditions, and, most important, our selves.

We are therapists in that we are committed to the health of individuals, families, groups, and social systems. As therapists, our focus may be on any part of the systems that impedes the quality of the interaction in and with the environment. Although we do not define ourselves by techniques, be they conventional or "alternative" techniques such as psychic healing, bodywork and imaging, we have come to believe that therapy must be holistic. It must fuse the mind-body-spirit and enhance one's ability to function as an individual within a collective group. It is our world view that defines how we work and how we view people, problems, situations, goals, and the appropriate focus and point of intervention.

A WORKSHOP

To demonstrate our perspective and to enable other practitioners to confront and correct biases in their practices, we offer a number of workshops for colleagues in the helping professions. One such workshop, designed for a group of white, presumably middle-class, professional women, is intended to demonstrate in an experiential manner that black women must contend with both racism and sexism simultaneously and that racial oppression cuts across sex and class-related issues.

At the beginning of the workshop, several members of SOURCE stand and then sit before the workshop participants. A moderator introduces us as members of SOURCE, but does not give our names or any other information about us as individuals. Participants are given a questionnaire to fill out independently, which asks the following questions:

- Which of the SOURCE members is easiest to "take in" and why?
- Which is furthest away from your image of a black woman and why?
- With whom would you go into therapy and why?
- Which of the SOURCE members is hardest to "take in" and why?
- Who most fits your image of a black woman and why?
- With whom would you like to take a course in economics, in black women's issues, or in clinical theory?
- With whom would you like to make love and why?
- Who would you like to have as a client and why?

The workshop builds on the fact that all people form impressions and judgments based on appearances, so questions are deflected by the moderator back to the participants until they have completed the questionnaires in writing. After some sharing of responses and discussion, participants are given autobiographical sketches of the women and asked to match the sketches with the group members. Because the women in the group differ from one another in class background, political orientation, mode of practice and setting, and the like, this exercise presents another opportunity to examine assumptions drawn from appearances.

The discussion focuses on the nature and sources of the assumptions. Patterned responses emerge quickly. Initially, reactions range from bewilderment to outrage and from "copping to prejudice" to vigorous denial. Insight and healing are promoted, however, by turning the discussion to an exploration of the structural roots of these reactions; gradually, participants are able to name those structures as racist, homophobic, elitist, classist, or patriarchal. More important, they are able to experience the ways in which those structures and supporting ideologies have shaped their experiences as well as the experiences of the black women. Moreover, their attempts to incorporate a visual image of a black woman into their personal and positive concepts of clinician, educator, lover, and favorite client suggests to the participants a new reality. The process enhances their ability to recognize in themselves the vitiating effects of oppressive ideologies while building their confidence in their ability to challenge these effects in their lives. In the tradition of consciousness raising, the process moves from confrontation to healing, from personal vulnerability through group sharing to political analysis and a commitment to act.

REFERENCES

1. Paul Horton and Chester Hunt, *Sociology* (2d ed.; New York: McGraw-Hill Book Co., 1968).

2. Alfred Pasteur and Ivory L. Tolson, *Roots of Soul: The Psychology of Black Expressiveness* (New York: Anchor Press, 1982).

MADONNA OF THE HILLS

She kept finding arrowheads
when she walked to Flower Mountain
and shards of ancient pottery
drawn with brown and black designs—
cloud ladders, lightning stairs and rainbirds.

One day
she took a shovel when she walked that way
and unburied fist-axes, manos, scrapers,
stone knives and some human bones,
which she kept in her collection
on display in her garden.

She said that it gave her
a sense of peace to dig and remember
the women who had cooked and scrubbed
and yelled at their husbands
just like her. She liked, she said,
to go to the spot where she'd found
those things and remember the women
buried there.

It was restful, she said,
and she needed rest—
from her husband's quiet alcohol
and her son who walked around dead.

PAULA GUNN ALLEN

manos—hand-held grinding stones.

From Geary Hobson, ed., *The Remembered Earth: An Anthology of Contemporary Native American Literature* (Albuquerque: University of New Mexico Press, 1981). Copyright © 1978 by Paula Gunn Allen. Reprinted by permission of the author.

MOTHER'S GLOWING EMBERS

yo
si sepo tu lumbre mamá
y lo senti cuando te lo pagaron
pero he left mother's embers
glowing
esta hija en tu matriz
y
i saw the wind coming over
singing songs to me
and she kissed mother's glowing embers
y si soy lesbiana mamá
tu lumbre burns *en esta hija*
porque vivo encantada
en tu matriz.

ARIBÁN

From *Bearing Witness/Sobreviviendo, CALYX: A Journal of Art and Literature by Women,* 8 (Spring 1984). Copyright © 1984 by Aribán. Reprinted by permission of the author.

Lesbians

MY MOTHER LOVES WOMEN

My mother loves women.

She sent me gold and silver earrings for Valentine's.
She sent a dozen red roses to Ruby Lemley
when she was sick and took her eight quarts
of purplehull peas, shelled and ready to cook.
She walks every evening down our hill and around
with Margaret Hallman. They pick up loose hub caps and talk
about hysterectomies and cataracts.
At the slippery spots they go arm in arm.

She has three sisters, Lethean, Evie, and Ora Gilder.
When they aggravate her she wants to pinch
their habits off like potatobugs off the leaf.
But she meets them each weekend for cards and jokes
while months go by without her speaking to her brother
who plays dominoes at the bus shop with the men.
I don't think she's known a man except this brother
and my father who for the last twenty years has been waiting
for death in his rocking chair in front of the TV set.

During that time my mother was seeing women
every day at work in her office. She knit them
intricate afghans and told me proudly
that Anne Fenton could not go to sleep without hers.

My mother loves women but she's afraid
to ask me about my life. She thinks
that I might love women too.

MINNIE BRUCE PRATT

A Rural and Lesbian Perspective on Feminist Practice

Pat L. Gunter

For this practitioner, who is a feminist and a lesbian in the rural South, "breaking silence" about who she was and what she believed was the beginning point of her work for social change. The author describes her work in developing networks in rural communities, including support groups for women who "come out" as lesbians in midlife and beyond, and a network of older gays and lesbians who provide counseling, support, and protection to adolescent gays and lesbians in small towns. Applied action research is another method used by the author to confront and change the interrelated conditions of sexism, racism, classism, and homophobia, in what is, in many ways, a feudal-agrarian social structure.

To be a feminist and a lesbian in a small southern rural community is both perilous and liberating. When the dimension of being a "woman identified woman" with a professional practice in the same environment is added, one encounters further barriers. Living and practicing in the rural environment has been not only a professional challenge but at times a personal challenge to survival. Both personal and professional battles against sexism, racism, classism, ageism, and homophobia are still major issues that need confronting if nonrewarding human conditions are to be changed.

Rural environments and their diverse populations often have been the focus of special attention by those in and related to the social work profession. This attention has generated a number of professional disagreements centered on the similarities and differences between urban and rural values, attitudes, needs, problems, and methods of service delivery. Another side of the argument has been the attempt to capture the virtues and positive aspects of rural populations, such as strong individualism, self-sufficiency, the ability to adapt, and the acceptance of diversity (if that diversity has

Pat L. Gunter, Ph.D., is a social work educator and community activist in southern Illinois. Her special interest is women's relationship to the land.

been a product of a specific rural environment). A much more realistic approach would be to accept that rural environments are a combination of both positive and negative aspects and work toward changing what can be changed by building on the strengths that have been identified as unique to any given region, community, or population. A major focus should be on how any individual's ability to function as an integrated, productive human being is affected by the personal and professional environment. This focus applies to the lesbian-feminist social work practitioner as well as to the populations to be served. The issues pertaining to women and lesbians in the rural environment have received little professional attention.

This article attempts to chronicle the process by which one rural social worker began to incorporate a personal lesbian-feminist perspective into rural practice. To develop a framework for a practice perspective, it is important to understand how one's personal self evolves into a lesbian-feminist and the integration of that personal self into a practitioner. To illustrate the process, I have presented my early experiences that helped to shape my philosophy of social work practice and have provided examples of how this philosophy is translated into actual direct and indirect service elements. Finally, I have topically outlined a framework that may be useful in self-examination or in providing guidance and direction to those who share similar concerns and problems.

DEVELOPING A LESBIAN-FEMINIST PERSPECTIVE

My early years, from childhood to adulthood, influenced the process by which I "came out" professionally. Those experiences, internal and external, provided the foundation for the emergence of a lesbian and a feminist, who, by choice, still lives and works in a rural environment and who realized that my choice of lifestyle has not only an effect on my practice but provides me with an opportunity to serve as a social-political activist.

I was adopted at age 5, along with a sister who was 3 years and a brother just over 1 year, by a married, childless couple in their early sixties. We three had been deserted by our natural parents in a small, primarily rural, midwestern community. Our foster parents had spent most of their lives in the community, helping to raise numerous children of other relatives during the depression years. Their major concern at the time of our adoption was to live long enough to see us through high school and as independent as possible. Not only did they accomplish this goal, but mother saw my completion of two master's degrees and father celebrated the awarding of my doctorate. Even though these two individuals were so much older when they began to raise a family, the generation gap was not as important as the love, support, and knowledge that they provided. In all aspects, it was a nontraditional, poor, rural, educated, midwestern farm family with a strong sense of the work ethic, respect for diversity, and encouragement of individuality.

The community was and is similar to thousands of others scattered throughout the Midwest. With a population of just over 7,000, it was economically dependent on the soft-coal industry and small farming. My parents had a place in the community because their family had helped settle the county. They were religious in a nontraditional sense, believing that good deeds were more reflective of religious ethics than was formal church membership; their outlook included a respect for all living things and a belief that each person has a place according to nature's laws.

My mother spent 32 years serving the county school system in a variety of one- and two-room schools. My father, a small farm operator, supplemented his income with various odd jobs, including work as a substitute mail carrier. Between the farm products, a small earned income, and later social security benefits, we managed well—not with frills or by today's standards, but with more-than-adequate supplies to meet our needs.

Family-style discussions often centered on historical events and the participation of my parents in attempting to bring about social change. They had a strong commitment to the principles and values of an egalitarian philosophy. Early stories reflected their reformist efforts on behalf of voting rights for women, unionization, and equal pay and work opportunities. My parents were early role models whom all three of us tried to emulate. Raised in an atmosphere that practices recognition and respect for diversity and that emphasizes the need to challenge and change the status quo, one realizes the importance of action in contrast to passive disagreement.

Specific gender-related roles were not a luxury that the family unit could afford. Regardless of gender, certain activities and tasks were necessary for survival, and all members were expected to contribute how and where they could. It was not unusual for my father to wash clothes, cook meals, iron, clean the house, and nurture us when we needed comfort. Nor was it unusual for my mother to help with the farm work, haying, building fences, cleaning wells, and roofing the house. They simply did not stress that certain roles were gender specific; rather, they emphasized that we were to learn skills, knowledge, and values that would help us to survive. After I reached adulthood, father told me of their concerns as parents of three young children when they were in the so-called later years of their life. He often spoke of having to grow with us and, to the day he died, he swore that his longevity was based on the day-to-day trials and joys of raising three small children. He also told me that both he and mother were aware of my "difference" in sexual orientation long before I shared my revelation with them.

Awareness of My Differences

When did I know I was a lesbian? Long before there were words to describe or attach a name to my difference in my child's mind. The full realization struck me when I was confronted with the "other" world, specifically the school system and the community at large. Although farm community tomboys are readily accepted, there still are limits placed on their behavior. To be rough and tough and ready for action is one thing, but to be aggressive and assertive, and to "moon" over other girls and women during elementary school is frowned on. Disapproval does not come so much from the various love objects, who seem to like the attention, but from other behavior watchers and self-appointed societal monitors.

Not only was I reprimanded by various behavior watchdogs, but concerns and even some complaints were directed to my parents. Although both parents wanted to protect me, they saw the need to focus several family and individual discussions on socially accepted patterns of behavior and the consequences of violating those rules. They did not attempt to change my behavior or to establish a set of rules to govern my growing-up years, but they tried to help me understand who I was and take responsibility for my actions, realizing that hurt, pain, and healing were a part of the process.

The phase of puberty and secondary school was one of the most painful and loneliest of my growing up. There were many confrontations and episodes that affected later relationships with family members, educational and religious systems, and the community. The offenses were such that I was considered guilty by probable cause, which reflected what I had the potential to do, not what I actually did. These offenses included such minor violations as having my love poems to another girl discovered, upsetting the minister's daughter in Sunday School so she could not concentrate on her lessons, being thrown out of church camp for being caught in bed with another girl (we were only talking), not being allowed to associate with certain girls in the community because of their parents' attitudes, and the blow of all blows, having to leave the Girl Scouts.

Being the proud possessor of an alternative sexual orientation can create havoc in a small rural community that is not tolerant of adolescent diversity. I experienced intense personal pain and internal conflict. Two major events brought into focus the duality of existence that "different" individuals often feel: (1) criticism from the community for my stance and verbalization of human rights and the need to take action against the prevalent "isms" at the time and (2) being denied the opportunity to participate in an essay contest on the virtues of being an American. My behavior was most often viewed as outrageous and certainly atypical of small-town individuals, and I developed a strong sense of the inequality and unfairness of that community.

At that time, my parents decided to have their most serious talk with me; even today, it is still hard to remember what took place without reexperiencing the love and the pain. By that point, I was well read and was certain, without a doubt, that I was a lesbian, a radical, and just possibly a communist. I knew that I was sick and needed therapy or at least to be saved by the church, that I needed perhaps even to get married and engage in sex, in that order, and to prepare myself for the revolution by studying Russian.

At the age of 16, I knew that I could not be open, that I could not change people, and that the burden I had placed on my family could not go on. Essentially my decision was to "recloset" myself and bide my time.

Two Self-Images

Before entering college, I had two self-images—one that reflected myself in terms of my parents and some supportive peers and adults and the other that reflected what I perceived was the perception of the "real world" (strangers), which was negative. At that time, I made every attempt to resolve the two images or to live two different lives, one for the world and one that was in my mind and heart. Mother and father helped me to resolve part of the conflict. During several intense discussions, two points were made clear. First, they stressed that one's life cannot be led by others' expectations but that each individual has to set his or her own life and then be responsible for it. They realized and accepted my lesbian nature and that the choice to live openly would be difficult and would require exceptional strength and courage. Second, my father impressed on me that the only real "sin" is feeling guilty because that guilt reflects the harm we have done to ourselves or to others. The outcome of this discussion provided a basis for a philosophy that still is very much my personal attitude toward others and life.

My high school academic record was excellent, and I obtained a scholarship to a small university only one hour away from my home town. College provided the setting in which my energies could be directed into action. It was a time to broaden my perspectives and to begin to identify with other women who either were searching or had consciously decided to abandon the traditional roles ascribed by society. The campus at that time also was a place where changes were taking place. It was growing, and the concept of *parentis in loco* was being challenged; stepping out of traditional models acceptable for women, identifying with other vulnerable groups, and going beyond conceptual intellectualism to action were being stressed. Even in the changing conservative atmosphere of the late 1950s, the professional person I was to become emerged and almost became fully liberated.

New-Found Freedom

The new-found freedom brought to the surface feelings of anger and frustration. Now I had a better understanding of the anger and a need to take action on a social-political level to bring about change. Idealistically, many of us charged forth without a full realization of the consequences. Demonstrations, sit-ins, "discuss-ins" not only brought confrontation with the university administration but also with various forms of local law enforcement agencies. In our senior year, several of us were suspended from the university and were not to be on the campus. Later, we petitioned to be allowed to complete our courses, promising to graduate and never to darken the halls again. Several of the women, including me, were required to seek professional services from the school psychiatrist. Each week, the psychiatrist would report our progress to the dean of women, who then duly informed various instructors that we could continue in our classes. The psychiatrist refused to deal with my emerging feminism or my open lesbianism. Her response to the situation was a prescription for Valium and the suggestion that I "grin and bear it." She apparently failed to realize that "bearing it with a grin" was the major part of the problem.

During the last semester of college, a wonderful event took place: I fell in love, and the love was reciprocated by a young woman with a background similar to mine and with many of the same commitments. The decision to live openly was mutually agreed on, as was the concept of making a life for ourselves in a more liberal environment. We picked the largest, most exciting city we could think of—New York. The move to New York was exciting, frightening, and at times traumatic. We had no contacts, no money, and few skills to deal with an environment that was not only alien but often hostile. Somehow we survived and, in the process, became stronger individuals, although the relationship did not last. After five years, we went our separate personal ways but, strangely, our professional paths have been similar, both in social work and in our involvement in the feminist movement.

Emergence as a Lesbian-Feminist Social Worker

The years in New York added the final dimension to my emergence as a lesbian-feminist social worker. Professional and personal experiences solidified and put into perspective some short- and long-term goals. Those ten years in New York helped me to become more self-assured, sensitive, and aware of myself as a rural person. Somehow, I never lost that sense of rurality and identification as a person of the land. The 1960s was a time of social change and sensitizing this country to the inequities of the system. It was a time of confrontation and challenge, a time to look ourselves over and to attempt to change what we did not like.

The exciting years of the late 1960s and the early 1970s in New York also brought about my total involvement in social-political activities. I became an activist. The activities led me into conflict not only with my hiring agency but with various units of law enforcement agencies. These encounters led to several arrests on a variety of different charges: congregating with known deviants (because of my presence during a raid on an after-hours gay-lesbian bar), disturbing the peace (in an attempt to organize voter registration in a southern state) civil disobedience (for participating in an antiwar demonstration), and being detained in a Third World country (for attempting to obtain information on the health status of women and children). I would not take back these encounters for anything; they have given me valuable experience in living and lessons in life that have helped shape my professional activities and that will continue to have an impact on everything I do and how I perceive my world and my professional service.

The choice to return and work in a rural environment was not done on the spur of the moment, but through an examination of values and beliefs and how these could best be utilized along with acquired skills and knowledge to bring about social change. It was easy with an integrated personal and professional identity to return to work with populations that were underserved. I realized, however, that to bring about change, I would need to live "openly" and to listen and act on what was being said rather than on my own need to initiate change. In addition, I needed to undersand what was happening and to know the various boundaries and operational limits of rural systems. I had no doubt that my personal life, my integrity, and my professional capabilities were going to be challenged, yet I felt that I had to make the effort.

There were choices in terms of the concept of "openness"; such decisions as "how open, with whom, and where?" all had to be considered. "Openness" has come to symbolize not only a personal lifestyle but professional practice. Drawbacks exist, but what is much more important are the skills to turn what might be a disadvantage into advantages that are consistent with my personal and professional philosophy.

LESBIAN-FEMINIST PRACTICE SETTING

The choice to practice as a lesbian-feminist in a rural environment was conscious and deliberate. It was a move to incorporate a feminist social-political philosophy into action, thus providing a framework for practice. How best to address this integration involves another level of decision. To initiate and produce change and to be an effective change agent, it is necessary to examine practice methods, strategies, populations, and levels of practice and to identify a setting to serve as the stage for service delivery. Knowledge, values, and skills are other areas that must be realistically assessed. A variety of service units in the public and private sectors can provide the rural social worker with many opportunities. This view is more difficult with lesbian-feminist practice. If at all possible, a combination of the two will provide ample opportunities, allowing the practitioner to develop accountability professionally, as well as a personal professional network that will permit independent action.

Advantages of a Public Agency

In a rural area, one advantage to working through the auspices of a public agency is increased visibility. Professional providers of services in rural areas must, by necessity, network for professional support. The practitioner also becomes part of the formal system. Another positive aspect of employment in a public agency is the need to travel throughout an area to provide or assess the need for services, which gives one the opportunity to build relationships between other providers of services and to form contacts with the informal systems. The rural lesbian-feminist social worker is a generalist in every sense. She assesses needs and carries out tasks while clearly defining the roles of educator, advocate, enabler, activist, administrator, and researcher. Research skills are invaluable when attempting to be a change agent.

Initial contacts on lesbian-feminist issues and concerns are best approached through knowledge and utilization of an informal system. Not only do feminist support systems operate in rural environments, but it is important that the practitioner be accepted into the system. The informal system must be assured that its personal code of behavior will not be violated.

Becoming familiar with and operational in the formal and informal system is a method of assessing the types of available services, the quality of services, specific gaps in services, and agency policies. This information can be the framework in which the worker develops training programs or awareness programs or it can be used to effect policy and administrative changes.

Discrimination in Service Delivery

Involvement with the lesbian/feminist network made me aware of the active discrimination in the provision of social services. For example, administrators and supervisors of a community mental health center do not like to be presented with documentation on the denial of services to a lesbian couple. They do not like to be told that crisis intervention workers are not handling calls from gays and lesbians. The director of a women's shelter has difficulty refuting that her staff and trained volunteers do not want to serve lesbians, women of color, and women over age 65. These are not random examples; such situations occur over and over again with little being done to correct them. To recognize that these situations occur is good, but to let them pass and not attempt to resolve them is professional neglect; often, this neglect is intentional as well as a product of fear.

Lesbian-feminist practice has in many ways succeeded not only in expanding services but in affecting the broader issues of attitudes and discrimination. An important role that the feminist practitioner can assume is that of an educator. In my private practice, as well as under the auspices of the university for which I work, time is made available for awareness groups, in-service training workshops, and community education. It is important first to sensitize workers to specific issues and concerns and to breakdown the myths and stereotypes of homosexuality. The individual practitioner should be able to call on others to help in the training process. I have utilized other professionals and volunteers effectively by being a trainer of trainers, in other words, using my expertise to prepare others to reach and work with much larger community groups in developing awareness and support groups and in serving as resource persons.

There are two advantages to the use of community leaders as trainers: the identification of the individual with the community and the community's acceptance of that person. These individuals do not need to be lesbian, gay, or feminist, but they should have certain characteristics of a leader, have correct information, and understand the issues and dynamics. This type of utilization also provides quick positive intervention when time and travel would be prohibitive to the professional practitioner.

Gay and Lesbian Youths

In my work in rural areas, I have found that, in almost every small community, at least one youth (if not more) has been identified as being a homosexual by a family member, minister, teacher, or peers. It was obvious that a program was needed that would provide information and guidance through a difficult developmental stage. The information that was available was so outdated and of such poor quality that it would be impossible for a youth to develop a positive self-image. Many youths expressed a feeling of isolation, problems at school, depression, and concern that they were mentally ill. Several in the original group had either attempted suicide or had contemplated suicide at one time or another.

Two plans were developed that addressed both the informational needs and the supportive needs of the youths. The first was to encourage libraries and the school system to update their published materials and to provide information to rural health clinics and adolescent health services. Another part to the first action was to sensitize teachers, ministers, physicians, and nurses to deal with the situation and to provide appropriate referrals to staff members of a social service agency who had been trained to deal with the concerns or perceived problems of these young people.

The second plan was to identify a group of older gays and lesbians who lived in the local communities and who were willing to act as role models and advocates for individual youths. This step is not particularly difficult if the worker has established a solid informal networking system. The advocates are screened, go through a period of training, and utilize the professional practitioner on an ongoing basis. The youths are screened by the social worker to assess their needs and how these needs can best be met. They are then assigned to an older advocate, much in the same manner as in the Big Brother–Big Sister programs. The personal and helping characteristics of the older advocate are important ingredients of this type of program. I have found that the most successful advocates are over age 45 and have been long-time residents of the community or have resided in the community long enough to have a respected role. Many have been or are "semicloseted"; they have lived a different lifestyle but have adhered to the standards of the community and have been accepted. The program currently operates primarily on an informal basis, with word of mouth being the primary referral mechanism.

A final aspect of this program has been the development of various support groups for parents, relatives, and friends of the youths. Again, these groups are conducted by trained volunteers. they are held as needed, often in various small churches in the area. Some of the involved parents become the first contact for other parents or relatives who are concerned about their children and themselves.

The role of the practitioner has been to develop and implement the various components of the program. After ten years of operation, it seems that the formal-informal approach of the program has met with less opposition from the community and from individuals than the more formal agency-conducted services. Two factors appear to have influenced the success of the program: (1) the use of informal leaders known to the community and (2) the absence of a formal agency. The latter may be the key factor because many of the state agencies have a negative image in the various communities.

Other Clients

Other groups of individuals that have been the focus of my practice include women who have been married, usually with children, who have now decided that they want to live openly as lesbians. Some are willing to come out completely, while others prefer to live in a semicloseted state. This practice has provided an opportunity not only for individual intervention, but for intervention with larger systems in both the public and private sectors. These women often are without skills or alternative resources and have difficulty with interpersonal relationships. They are highly vulnerable and need as much support as possible. The majority of cases need individual treatment as well as an easily accessible support system. The role of the worker is to aid in educating, advocating for, and strengthening a particular individual.

The aged and those who have taken refuge in a dependency on drugs and alcohol are two other major concerns. Rural areas have a high proportion of aged people; in many counties, the percentage of the population aged 60 and over is as high as 42 percent. Because of differences in the life span of men and women in this age group, the majority of the rural aged are women. The access of elderly people to services and resources is limited and presents unique concerns and issues for the rural social work feminist practitioner. Rather than even attempting to develop specific plans for each individual, the practitioner must deal with the service systems, challenging not only the policies and awareness of agencies but those state and federal policies that actively discriminate against rural populations. The primary focus of this intervention is to have an impact on administration and policymakers. In this case, research is an excellent tool; collecting, analyzing, and presenting empirical data can change the way in which guidelines are developed and implemented. Community or grass-roots developmental tools also bring about changes in the system.

Relationship to Colleges and Universities

Another task facing the rural lesbian-feminist social worker is to act as a change agent in the traditional male-oriented heterosexual academic setting. The policies, curricula, and resources of universities and community colleges do not address the diverse needs of the student populations, especially women, lesbians, the aged, and minorities of color. Nor is the status of women and lesbians high in academic settings. Although this problem is not unique to rural environments, the roles played by institutions of higher education are unique. A particular academic system may be viewed not only as an educational institution but as a major source of information and help, as well as the provider of cultural and socialization activities. The presence of the lesbian-feminist practitioner in such institutions should be felt, and her contributions should be recognized and rewarded. The easiest way to do so is to be a guest lecturer in various courses in which women's issues and lesbianism are taught. The next step is to push for the expansion of information on women's issues and lesbianism in various subject areas. Many faculty members are willing to do so if they have the materials and some guidance and support in preparing the courses.

Finally, the lesbian-feminist practitioner can use her expertise on a larger scale by becoming politically active, not just in local politics, but on boards of agencies, advisory councils, local banks, and schools and in multidisciplinary service teams and women's centers. This type of activity not only creates visibility but it assures that the practitioner has input into various decision-making processes. Another example of political involvement, one that is most often ignored, is presenting testimony at hearings on policies that may lead to discriminatory legislation and the establishment of impossible guidelines. Although this activity may be time consuming and difficult, the practitioner should engage in it from personal and professional concern. Pending or suggested legislation may appear to affect only our clients or potential clients, but usually it influences our professional lives, which, in turn, disturbs our sense of personal well-being.

The decision to practice openly as a lesbian-feminist social worker does not come easily. The process I went through was both difficult and refreshing. The following guidelines for practice have been developed with the aid of many marvelous lesbian-feminist social workers who have expressed a need to bring their total selves to social work practice.

GUIDELINES FOR LESBIAN-FEMINIST PRACTICE

Identifying Specific Issues or Concerns

In the beginning, it is a good idea to address the following issues and concerns:

■ Our feelings about and choices of a lifestyle that we have in relation to our needs, desires, goals, and understanding of who and what we are or want to be.

■ The values, knowledge, and roles of practice, which set the stage for many of the actions and activities that come later as a result of defining our professional practice.

■ In integrating our practice and lifestyle, we begin to look at our awareness of self and our professional perceptions of self. This process often is a questioning phase and is the beginning of the integration of what might be two identities (personal and professional). Even though the two identities can be separated, it is important to know the reasons why and how effectively they work together for the unity of the individual. Integration does not mean a blurring of roles but, rather, the working together of one's various roles and sets of expectations.

■ The evaluation of self and practice is important in the establishment of personal and professional goals as well as in providing a mechanism that can help us to evaluate successes and failures. We may need to redefine our goals in terms of self and practice—to determine what is realistic and possible compared to what is idealistic.

Clarifying Lesbian-Feminist Roles in Practice

To realize fully the goals of effective lesbian-feminist practice in any environment, one must undergo a process through which a purposeful direction can be maintained. This can be accomplished by an examination of the various roles that a practitioner could assume and those elements of components that have an impact on a practitioner's performance. The elements to be considered are as follows:

■ Levels of practice (micro-macro).
■ Methods of practice.
■ Roles of practice (educator, broker, advocate, enabler, and so forth).
■ Skills, knowledge, values, and attitudes of practice in relation to the work environment and the populations to be served.
■ Choice of practice setting (private or public agencies, administration, policy and research, and so forth).

Ingredients in Lesbian-Feminist Practice

Other factors that need to be considered when one seeks to practice both as a personal and professional lesbian are these:

■ Which will be more effective: high visibility or low visibility?
■ Who are your personal and professional support systems, where are they, how do they operate, and how can you as a practitioner work with them?
■ The need for and intensity of various types of relationships, both personal and professional.
■ Your level of commitment—your strength, energy, and willingness to risk failure.
■ Your credibility as an individual and as a social worker within the lesbian-feminist framework.

CONCLUSION

Feminism is an ideology and as a social movement has had and will continue to have as much of an impact as any other social-political phenomenon on the direction that social work practice has taken or will take in the future. To identify how the lesbian-feminist practitioner functions within the practice setting depends on two factors that are difficult to separate. One factor is the personal, which really is a process by which an individual comes to terms with her lesbianism and feminism. The other factor is the professional—the incorporation of feminist principles and values into professional practice.

A lesbian practitioner who works within the concept of a feminist philosophy must view practice in terms of a process framework of integrated factors. Practice is belief, practice is action, and practice is political. Just as feminism is a social-political philosophy and ideology, so is lesbianism. The practicing lesbian-feminist social worker can personally and professionally be productive in advocating and initiating change on any level and still be committed to the integrity of the self as it reflects a global view of relationships with all living things.

As a practicing lesbian-feminist social worker in rural areas, I have and will continue to encounter a variety of issues that focus not only on my practice but on attitudes toward feminist thought, sexual orientation, and nontraditional relationships. The direction my practice assumes is constantly being called into question, including the legitimacy of my actions and personal or professional encounters. The choice to challenge larger systems professionally, such as education, social work, human service agencies, and political machines, has taken strength, determination, and a belief that the change that does occur enhances the quality of life of all human beings.

Much more needs to be done. How we resolve many of the problems is an individual decision based on the great diversity of women in social work. Yet that diversity is a great strength on which to build as women, feminists, lesbians, and professional social workers. Through sharing our beliefs, attitudes, knowledge, successes, and failures, we can contribute to a safer, saner world for everyone through a personal and professional commitment to serving those who do not have a representative voice.

TO CONFIRM A THING

To confirm a Thing and give thanks
                              to the stars that named me
and fixed me in the Wheel of heaven
                    my fate pricked out in the Boxer's chest
in the hips curled over the Horse
                    Though girled in an apple-pink month
and the moon hornless
                    the Brothers glitter in my wristbones
At ankle and knee I am set astride
                              and made stubborn in love

In the equal Night where oracular beasts
                              the planets depose
and our Selves assume their orbits
                    I am flung where the Girdle's double studs
grant my destiny
                    I am the Athletes in that zone
My thighs made marble-hard
                         uncouple only to the Archer
with his diametrical bow
                    who prances in the South
himself a part of his horse
                    His gemmed arrow splits the hugging Twins

The moon was gelded on that other night as well
                    Oh his feeble kingdom we will tip over
If our feet traverse the Milky Way
          the earth's eccentric bead on which we balance
is small enough to hide between our toes
                    its moon a mote that the Long Eye
is hardly conscious of
                              nor need we be
The tough the sensuous Body our belief
                    and fitting the pranks of Zeus
to this our universe
          we are Swans or Bulls as the music turns us
We are Children incorrigible and perverse
                    who hold our obstinate seats
on heaven's carousel
                    refusing our earth's assignment
refusing to descend
                    to beget such trifles as ourselves
as the gibbous Mothers do

We play in the den of the Gods
and snort at death

Then let me by these signs
                    maintain my magnitude
as the candid Centaur his dynasty upholds
                    And in the Ecliptic Year
our sweet rebellions
                    shall not be occulted but remain
coronals in heaven's Wheel

MAY SWENSON

Men & Feminist Practice

Love Poem to an Ex-Husband

You were always the one
I asked to kill things:
rabbits disembowelled by the cat,
quail with wings snapped and useless.
I called it mercy
until one day you refused.

I had found a tortoise
smashed like an egg by a tractor,
its shell cracked
and the yolk of its entrails
spread across the dusty road.
Still alive with pain and fear
it moved without moving
toward the refuge of some green shade.

It had to be ended
but you said *No.*
This time someone else
could do the killing.
So I shovelled it
into a bucket of water
and watched it
breathe in its death.

You had not acted like a man
and I never loved you better
than when I stood before the fragments,
in the fear and the necessity of action,
the breath of death and life.

I am separate now and far away,
yet sometimes I still stand with you
in the evening by the road
and watch the fireflies light the alders
in the dim green down beside the pond.

MINNIE BRUCE PRATT

Men and Feminist Practice

Philip Lichtenberg

Some take the position that men can be feminists but, because of their participation in the privileged structures of patriarchy, they cannot be nonsexist. Others say that men can learn to behave in nonsexist ways and participate in the construction of liberating structures, but cannot be feminists because feminism is rooted in women's unique experience as women. The Feminist Practice Project did not take a position on this, but sought to advance the dialogue by encouraging people to define themselves in their own terms. This article is by a male social worker who has openly identified himself as a feminist since being called one by women colleagues. He describes his work, which has been influenced by his feminism, in teaching, research, and psychotherapy. He emphasizes the dynamics of domination and "the unfolding of fusion between oppressors and the oppressed." ———*Editor's Note*

Some years ago, students who were organizing in the school of social work in which I teach created a feminist group (called "New World Women") and invited me to participate in promoting a feminist presence in the curriculum and in the school environment. Quite offhandedly, they said that, of course I was a feminist; being a man did not prevent me from being one, and they thought that the tenor of my commitments was qualification for that title. The students seemed to be making obvious sense in their remarks. Since that time, I have openly identified myself as a feminist, not simply as a man who is interested in women's issues.

ORIGINS OF MY FEMINISM

Addressing the origins for my feminism led me to three different sources: my social and political radicalism, my family history, and my ideological and theoretical convictions. I spent my childhood in a northern Indiana com-

Philip Lichtenberg, Ph.D., is a social work educator, psychotherapist, and radical political activist. At the Graduate School of Social Work and Social Research, Bryn Mawr College, Bryn Mawr, Pennsylvania, he has been active in a group of feminist educators who are seeking to promote a feminist presence in the social work curriculum and in the environment of the school.

munity that was reactionary—that considered an allegiance to President Franklin D. Roosevelt to be the ultimate in godless radicalism. I remember seeing a cross burned in the front yard of a friend of my family, and I still visualize myself standing on the outer rim of a mob of people who were screaming curses at a Jewish manager of a department store, whom they ultimately drove out of town. Hostility to black people was common in the city and openly displayed; I vividly recall picketing for civil rights in the 1940s. The German-American Bund was active, and American Nazis were visible and vocal in their support of Adolf Hitler.

Faced with this atmosphere, it was not hard for me to drift toward radicalism as I grew up. The nature of that radicalism was a strong commitment to democracy—not crude political democracy, but the practice of democratic principles in all the institutions of our lives—and thoroughgoing egalitarianism. I consider these principles to be native American commitments—social positions that were articulated in the textbooks at my schools and in the presumed ideology of the land. As with feminism, I did not know that I was a radical until someone told me that my insistence on democracy and equality made me one. Out of that firm devotion to the equality of people as a social and political stance came my assumption of the importance of equality between women and men, and hence my feminism.

The relationships in my family as I was growing up also disposed me toward feminism. My father was a social and political conservative, while my mother, with whom I identified in these matters, was liberal. My brother was a model for interest in sexuality, but my older sister, at least in the early years when my political ideas were taking shape, was a political person, and she introduced me to Paul Robeson, my childhood hero, to the Almanac Singers with Woody Guthrie and Pete Seeger, and to other left-wing political influences. These identifications probably contributed to my feminism. It has not hurt that my wife has been an active and effective feminist (as was my late mother-in-law).

My perspective on equality entered my research work at an early stage in my career. My first job was as a research fellow in clinical psychology at Harvard University, working in the world of Henry A. Murray on emotional maturity and mental health. (My greatest support in that world came from Tamara Dembo and Christiana Morgan, two superb thinkers and human beings.) In doing pilot work for a research experiment, I engaged my wife and mother-in-law in a small exercise. I asked that they independently create a plot for a drama; then I brought them together and asked them to design a new plot built on the productions each had done alone. I kept their individual stories and then tape-recorded their conversation when they were developing the new joint plot. From casual observation, it seemed clear that the final product made by their joint work was dominated by my mother-in-law, which did not surprise me. My mother-in-law was a powerful person, and although my wife was young and rebellious, she was at that time pregnant and seemed to prefer being taken care of in that new environment. You may imagine my surprise, then, when I analyzed, point by point, the final plot and discovered that my wife and mother-in-law had contributed *equally* to the outcome. What had seemed like simple dominance did not turn out to be inequality of contribution. Later, when I conducted the experiment with pairs of Harvard students, I found the same result. *Relationships among people*, I learned then, and have believed ever since (not always to the pleasure of my fellow feminists) are inevitably *relations of equals*. I was put onto the track of the Scottish philosopher John Macmurray, as a result of those early experiments and commend him to you for an informed view that equality reigns, even when people intend superiority and domination. My research in mental health, child rearing, and social struggles has carried that theme over the ensuing years. It is my ideological and theoretical bias.

IMPLICATIONS OF DOMINATION AND EXPLOITATION

Some implications of this ideological and theoretical perspective when domination and exploitation prevail in social relationships are as follows:

■ The costs to those in the more powerful position are greater than is usually assumed. If one looks closely, one finds comparable limitations for the oppressors and the oppressed. For example, although the material wealth of the managers in an industrial society is obviously greater than that of the workers, what about their psychological experience, their emotional gratifications? One usually just assumes that it is greater without looking closely. I have come to see it otherwise, to see the oppressors also as being oppressed. Relationships of exploitation lower the quality of life for all participants. The relationships of women and men are one domain in which this pattern of decreased gratification exists.

■ The oppressed participate in their own oppression. By now, this idea is almost conventional wisdom, and we must be certain that we are not blaming the victim when we make this observation. However, this common observation must be put into a theoretical framework. That relationships between people are always relationships of equals is exactly the theoretical linkage that is needed. Men gain equally when women are liberated and suffer equally when they attempt to dominate.

■ Oppression exists, but its meaning must now be redefined. When what we call oppression, domination, or exploitation is in effect, the intent is for some to gain while others sacrifice. Instead of these intentions being realized, the actual circumstance is that all participants in a relationship achieve lower levels of personal satisfaction. Oppression introduces indirection, dishonesty, self-conquest, and distrust, so that achievements necessarily decrease. Thus, "oppression" describes human relationships that are based on assumptions, perceptions, and intentions that violate the realities of human interaction, especially the reality that persons in a relationship necessarily act to equalize.

FEMINISM IN MY PRACTICE

Teaching

How does feminism enter my practice? My practice involves teaching, research, and psychotherapy. Feminism is implemented in my teaching in several ways. As was already mentioned, in the New World Women's project, my feminism was expressed through support of and involvement with that group of students. When the group was active, it was the most influential group in the school, invigorating the student government, which had fallen on hard times; instigating a Task Force on Women's Issues; and raising the consciousness of students and faculty through the development of several support groups. Participation in this group was perhaps the most direct and full expression of my feminism.

As a teacher, a second outlet has been the opportunity to serve as a mentor to doctoral students and to junior faculty members who are feminist in orientation. I have tried to foster in women doctoral students a sense of their possibility and responsibility as independent scholars, thinkers, and researchers who originate ideas as well as pass them along. I have supervised the dissertations of lesbian feminists, radical feminists, socialist feminists, and liberal feminists, as well as those who have no idea of their feminism but are women scholars. The students have worked on women's issues from a feminist perspective: the dialectics of nurturance, autonomy, and expectant dependence; abortion; views of women reflected in national legislation; the timing of having children in adult development; daughters and fathers; and so forth. I have consciously brought along students and junior faculty members as full collaborators in research projects in which I am engaged and have helped to establish them as important figures in the field.

A third outlet has been my classes on practice. For example, I teach a nonsexist orientation to psychoanalysis, which contains both basic psychoanalytic and radical social thought—an orientation that is attractive and surprising to feminist students. I introduce women's issues in my courses on personality theory, change and resistance to change, racial and ethnic perspectives, and policy and personality. Furthermore, my feminism is important as a support to women who resume their studies after having been out of school for a number of years. Many talented women in their mid-thirties, who have returned to school to prepare for a profession, challenge their families with their new autonomy. They commonly struggle with the problems of career and home, separateness in their marriages, and other such issues. They need and prosper under the proper support and appreciate when that support is provided, by a woman or a man.

Research

As I intimated previously, the matter of equality between people is woven into the research that I do. One such research topic is the mutual creation of oppression by the "weak" and the "strong" in what my colleagues and I have called "social-emotional keys to the division of power." We see the unfolding of fusion between oppressors and the oppressed through a combination of identification with the aggressor and what we have named "projection on a primed vulnerable other." (The origins of the useful concept of "identification with the aggressor," by the way, go back to studies in child abuse that Freud and Ferenczi carried out a long time ago.[1]) In our research, we carry forward the idea that equality exists (such as equality of satisfaction in events), even when it does not look like that could be the case. As you may imagine, or feel yourselves, feminists who think that women suffer more than men in direct relationships between the sexes do not always agree with this idea. However, when one looks from the perspective of equality, whether it concerns freedom in the external world, power in handling finances, or sexual relations, one sees different things than when one assumes otherwise and views relationships from the alternative perspective. It is necessary to look for gains and losses of everyone in such interactions. For example, in the previously mentioned experiment with my mother-in-law and my wife, it appeared that my mother-in-law took more from the experience than did my wife; yet, a close, exact analysis demonstrated that they took equally. Applying the same detailed assessment to relationships that seem as if one partner is dominant and the other submissive invariably, in my experience, reveals the prevalence of similar equality. Usually, however, we do not make the detailed assessment because we think the unequal division of satisfactions is obvious. I can only urge you to try out the idea; take a situation that looks heavily unequal and see if you can find the equalizing tendency and the resultant equality between the participants.

Psychotherapy

Lastly, feminism is integrated into my work as a psychotherapist. It appears in my work with men, in which I foster egalitarianism, attention to women's issues, sensitivity to social mores that lead to the oppression of women, awareness of the value of autonomy in women and nurturance and "expectant dependence" in men. Serving as a male feminist model for men who are clients, sometimes seen alone and sometimes as partners in couples, is a contribution of my feminism in psychotherapy. I work with women as well as men on an individual basis, and my feminism enters that practice too. The same values and theoretical perspectives that inform my teaching and my research are played out in these endeavors and make of my practice a "natural feminism," not a forced one. My closest co-workers in my practice of psychotherapy are feminists; hence, my referrals, consultations, supervision, and other ancillary activities are heavily influenced by and kept honest with respect to a feminist perspective.

Because my different areas of practice take place in contexts influenced by feminism, I am fortunate to have continuing demands from active feminists. Bryn Mawr College, where I teach, is known as a women's college, although its graduate schools have been coeducational for many years. My psychotherapy work is tied to the Gestalt Therapy Institute of Philadelphia, which is heavily influenced by its feminist leadership. My research is done in collaboration with feminist research associates, and my family, including my several daughters-in-law and my wife, is feminist too. I feel fortunate, indeed, by their surrounding presence.

REFERENCES

1.   Sander Ferenczi, *Sex in Psychoanalysis, 1911* (New York: Basic Books, 1950); and Sigmund Freud, *Collected Papers*, Vol. 5 (London, England: Hogarth Press, 1924).

every man for himself

we shall be brilliant
we shall collect data
we shall write books
about men
unhappiness
and bedrooms

we shall extol vulnerability
keep a loaded 45 within reach
kick ass when necessary
and get on with
the business of brotherhood

we shall make a key
it will open the door
there will be no house

we are the scholars
of the fast break
and the full court press

SIDNEY MILLER

From *Play the Melody: Poems by Sidney Miller* (Fort Lee, N.J.: Time Out Press, 1983).

Spirituality
&
Healing

HOW TO MAKE A GARDEN IN THE CITY

Go for a walk. Look for weeds.
Learn which you can eat.
Eat them.
Walk the train tracks;
look for what falls off.
Use it.
Find yourself a pot;
put a little dirt in it.
Find some old leaves, look for worms beneath.
Add them all to the pot,
and eggshells, onion skins, leftover tea.
Give the worms some time to work.
Plant something.
Do it again
and again.

Every morning touch the earth.
Every night praise the worms.
Listen.

CATHERINE RISINGFLAME MOIRAI

First appeared in *Feminary*, Vol. 12, No. 1 (1982). Copyright © 1982 by Catherine Risingflame Moirai. Reprinted by permission of the author.

A Psychic/Physical Healer Perspective on Feminist Practice

Phyllis A. Maass
Harriet L. Cohen

The reclamation of traditional healing arts and the integration of mind, body, and spirit are enduring themes in the women's movement. They have led many practitioners to the study of alternative and sometimes ancient healing arts, including psychic healing, massage, and other forms of body work; imaging; meditation; spiritualism; rituals; and witchcraft. The authors of this article turned to "energistic healing" in their search for more effective, wholistic methods. They describe why and how they combined this method with the influences of their feminist political orientation and their combined 30 years' experience practicing social work in a psychosocial tradition.

The approach of social workers working from this model is analogous to that of Judy Chicago in the collective creation of The Dinner Party: *"[The work] represents the fusion of women's ideas from the context traditionally associated with women—that is, needlework—to the context traditionally associated with men—painting. It is this infusion of the whole stream of women's history and. . .into the structure of civilization that* The Dinner Party *is all about. By introducing the achievements of these women, by representing their containment, we will understand the way in which women's experience has been left outside of the mainstream of Western civilization. And my dream is that their experience as represented in this work of art will become part of and incorporated into our future, which will thereby be enriched."[1]*
———*Editor's Note*

We are social workers who have had over 30 collective years' experience in social work practice and education. Although for many years we were interested in such people as John Lilly and R. D. Laing, who examined life from a nontraditional stance, we did not embrace the practical aspects of exploring alternative approaches to mind-body integration until the early 1980s.[2]

Phyllis A. Maass, MSW, and Harriet L. Cohen, Ph.D., are both former social work educators who now practice and conduct training workshops for other women in the health and mental health professions in Georgia.

As a result of experiencing physical conditions that did not respond to traditional medicine, we became interested in health-care alternatives that initially included nutritional and vitamin therapy, massage, chiropractic, and applied kinesiology. These alternative approaches often are lumped together as "holistic health" practices. In 1981, we departed from social work practice and education, looking for theory and practice that offered more than a maintainence of the status quo, that is, adjustment to the accepted mode of thinking, behaving, and feeling that has been defined by the masculine values of law and order.

We began to build and incorporate a model of "holistic health" into our practice and teaching, using the holistic view that when all parts of the person—body, mind, spirit, and emotions—are balanced, then the person is expressing full health. The emphasis in holistic health is on health and well-being, not just on the absence of disease.[3]

ENERGISTIC HEALING

In discussing energistic healing (hands-on healing), we refer to the use of physical energy, which surrounds each of us as an electromagnetic field (as demonstrated by Kirlian photography) being used to balance the life force of another living being. We are not referring to the use of magic or mystical powers but, rather, to the use of the life force that is an animating current of life and is consciously directed by the enabler to facilitate the balancing of the other person. With energistic healing, the three main types of awareness—physical, emotional, and intellectual—can be brought together to work positively to create more complete health or balance. Spiritual awareness develops when the physical, mental, and emotional aspects of one's being are in harmony.[4]

Our introduction to hands-on healing was through a man and a woman who had organized a church in which they were ordained ministers to achieve the necessary sanction to provide hands-on healing, which is regulated in many states. As we mentioned earlier, we had already begun to explore alternatives to traditional medicine. After a didactic introduction, with hesitation and with many questions, we became involved as "patients". Even with our social work training and experience, we were unprepared for the dramatic and intense results produced by the hands-on healing, which works directly with blocks in various parts of the body, releasing attitudes formed by individual, family, and cultural socializing experiences. Working directly with the energy of the life force produces more accelerated results than are achieved with traditional psychotherapy.

We realized that practitioners (sometimes called "healers," although one can only cure oneself) of alternative treatment modalities emphasize the release of blocks or tensions, defined as attitudes, within oneself. However, such practitioners often are not prepared to lend necessary support to resolve the issues that arise from their work. Our concern, from an experiential and a theoretical perspective, stems from these practitioners' lack of knowledge of human behavior and of the helping process and from their failure to recognize that the blocks or tensions often represent defense mechanisms that developed as a result of the person's experience of her individual, family, and cultural scripting. Moreover, without a feminist perspective to help interpret what is happening, women are often encouraged to embrace the limited patriarchal values of the role and function of women in this society that are causing conflict and which women are trying to resolve. These concerns led us to attempt to integrate and synthesize energistic healing, feminism, and social work.

INTERFACE OF EASTERN PHILOSOPHY AND FEMINIST SOCIAL WORK

Eastern philosophy and healing practices interface on several levels with a feminist social work perspective and can promote feelings of independence and power in women as they reclaim their healing powers. The feminist orientation and the Eastern philosophy of communal sharing of responsibility moves women away from personal isolation, which is fostered by the structure of the nuclear family and of the larger society, to a sensitivity to the shared problems that are related to social conditions.[5] From sharing personal struggles, women can recognize what they need to heal in themselves as women and in society. Our work in practice and training has focused on helping women identify areas of conflict based on individual, family, and cultural scripts and on resolving negative attitudes that inhibit positive healing and growth. By recognizing the discordance between a woman's individual goals and desires and society's goals for women, women can begin to build alliances for strength and support, defining health in positive collective terms.

We have combined Oriental and Western healing systems with feminist practice, emphasizing enhancement of the relationship between one's inner and outer world and allowing for individual diversity. We stress certain universal principles: we all are responsible for creating those relationships and situations in which we find ourselves, based on our socialization and life experiences; wellness is more than the absence of "dis-ease"; we have the power to contribute to healing ourselves; and we are continually creating our realities. As facilitators (all people are their own healers if they chose) in energistic healing, we focus on preventive care, natural treatments, and personal responsibility of each woman for her own health. We see healing as the channeling of love and loving as the channeling of healing energy. We apply these principles in our practice of hands-on healing and in the training seminars we offer to other women.

In a patriarchal society, the masculine values (sometimes referred to somewhat inclusively as the "yang" energy of society) of rational thought, personal power, and law and order are emphasized. Men assume dominant roles at the expense of feminine energy (conversely referred to as the "yin" energy of society). Traditional mental health practice may be viewed as an instrument of this patriarchal society because it emphasizes adjusting and adapting to the limited role defined for women.

In a matriarchal society, female values emphasize the laws of instinct and nature, of feeling and emotion, of receptivity, and of sensitivity to the cyclical nature of life. The energistic approach to health emphasizes a balance of the yin-yang energies that integrate the physical, emotional, intellectual energies and create individual balance. The change from yin to yang to yin to yang is cyclic and continuous for individuals, in Nature, and in the world in which we live. One cannot exist without the other. In Oriental philosophy, to label yin or yang as good or bad, as destructive or constructive (as desirable or not desirable) is to reject half of existence. It denies the *Tao,* or "all that is." Such denial is to negate the dynamic principle of change. The dual forces of yin and yang interact as complementary opposites, revealing that things exist in relation to their opposites and that together they form a whole. Some of each element of the yin-yang force is found in its complementary opposite. Women need to claim their female (yin) energies and to create new ways of integrating and balancing the feminine and masculine energies within them. They need to develop a yin-yang balance to be complete. Conversely, men need to balance their energies to be able to cease enslaving women's feminine energies for their completion.[6]

All people are born into this world with the potential to be whole and integrated human beings. If their demands are met with nurturance, love, and understanding as infants, they have the capacity to develop normal healthy bodies. However, if their needs are not met with genuine support and care, they will begin to create tensions and physical blocks to deaden the impulses that lead to feelings of fear and rejection. Young children often develop patterns in response to family and cultural demands, which they continue to use unconsciously as adults. By releasing the tensions created over the years through energistic healing and other therapies, they also release the unresolved feelings that were blocked.

According to Oriental philosophy, "dis-ease" is the result of the blockage or stagnation of energy through the energy meridians, which correspond to the internal organs. The 12 organ meridians are the lungs, large intestines, stomach, spleen, heart, small intestines, bladder, kidneys, pericardium, triple warmer (which governs the production of energy), gall bladder, and liver. The yin organ meridians, which generally travel along the front of the body, are the spleen, liver, kidneys, lungs, pericardium, and heart. The yang meridians, going along the back and through the head, are the stomach, gall bladder, bladder, large intestines, triple warmer, and the small intestines. Each organ meridian is traditionally associated with particular physical, mental, and emotional functions.[7]

Just as there exists a yin-yang interaction that applies to Nature, so there is a yin-yang interaction that applies to one's physical being and can be brought into harmony by balancing the yin-yang energies channeled through the organ meridians. The following is a personal example of the use of healing techniques to balance the yin-yang interaction:

> One of the authors had functioned "successfully" for many years in the male professional and social world. Despite having supported other causes and movements, she never became intimately involved in the feminist movement and frequently commented to that effect. Through the physical unblocking process, working directly with balancing the yin and the yang meridians, attitudes came to the surface that necessitated that she face having identified herself with the male values of our society and, thus, as having viewed women who did not "make it" in that world as inadequate. Out of those realizations (those newly incorporated attitudes) came a growing sense of the injustice of the patriarchal system and of an identification with the women's movement. She no longer has to function as "one of the boys," denying feminine aspects of herself. Her yin-yang energies are more balanced since the blocks were released, which allows the life force to flow more freely.

Because of our personal experience with a healer who had a patriarchal view of society, we felt a commitment and responsibility to expand our feminist philosophy and apply it to our growing skill in energistic healing. We are still discovering how to integrate the use of touch and direct physical contact with social work practice. However, we think there is a strong need for feminist practitioners to provide support and therapy to clients in dealing with attitudes brought to the surface through any of the various healing techniques. The feminist orientation of communal sharing of responsibility moves us away from the personal isolation encouraged by the structure of the nuclear family to a sensitivity to shared problems we face as women living in a patriarchal society.

In sum, our work with women in practice and education now focuses on helping women identify areas of personal conflict based on individual, family, and cultural scripts, on resolving those conflicts, and on recognizing and reclaiming the healing powers women possess as individuals and as a collective.

REFERENCES

1. Judy Chicago, closing statement from Acoustiguide audiotape of *The Dinner Party*. Copyright © 1980 by Judy Chicago. Used by permission.

2. John Lilly, *Center of the Cyclone* (New York: Crown Publishers, 1972); Lilly, *Lilly on Dolphins* (New York: Crown Publishers, 1975); R. D. Laing, *The Politics of Experience* (New York: Pantheon Books, 1967); and Laing, *the Politics of the Family and Other Essays* (New York: Pantheon Books, 1971).

3. See, for example, Allen Marcus and Shakti Gawain, *Reunion: Tools for Transformation, A Guide to Meditation and Relaxation* (rev. ed.; Mill Valley, Calif.: Whatever Publishing, 1978); Berkeley Holistic Health Center, *Holistic Health Handbook: A Tool for Attaining Wholeness of Body, Mind, and Spirit* (Berkeley, Calif.:

And / Or Press, 1978); Tracy Deliman and John S. Smolowe, eds., *Holistic Medicine: Harmony of Body, Mind, Spirit* (Reston, Va.: Reston Publishing Co., 1982); George Downing, *The Massage Book* (New York: Random House, 1972); and Roberta DeLong Miller, *Psychic Massage* (New York: Harper Colphon Books, 1975).

4. Richard Gordon, *Your Healing Hands: The Polarity Experience* (Mill Valley, Calif.: Orenda Publishing / Unity Press, 1978); and Delores Krieger, *The Therapeutic Touch: How to Use Your Hands to Help or to Heal* (Englewood Cliffs, N.J.: Prentice-Hall, 1979).

5. Swami Rama et al., *Yoga and Psychotherapy: The Evolution of Consciousness* (Honesdale, Pa.: Himalayan Institute of Yoga, Science & Philosophy, 1976).

6. Mary Daly, Gyn / Ecology: *The Metaethics of Radical Feminism* (Boston: Beacon Press, 1978); Diane Mariechild, *Mother Web: A Feminist Guide to Psychic Development* (Trumansberg, N.Y.: Crossing Press, 1981); Anica Vesel Mander and Anne Kent Rush, *Feminism As Therapy* (New York: Random House, 1974); and Amy Wallace and Bill Henkin, *The Psychic Healing Book* (New York: Dell Publishing Co., 1978).

7. Ron Kurtz and Hectora Prestera, *The Body Reveals: An Illustrated Guide to the Psychology of the Body* (New York: Harper & Row, 1976).

TESTIMONY

There's godlike
And warlike
And strong
Like only some show
And there's sadlike
And madlike
And had
Like we know
but by my life be I spirit
And by my heart be I woman
And by my eyes be I open
And by my hands be I whole

They say slowly
Brings the least shock
But no matter how slow I walk
There are traces
Empty spaces
And doors and doors of locks
but by my life be I spirit
And by my heart be I woman
And by my eyes be I open
And by my hands be I whole

You young ones
You're the next ones
And I hope you choose it well
Though you try hard
You may fall prey
To the jaded jewel
But by your lives be you spirit
And by your hearts be you women
And by your eyes be you open
And by your hands be you whole

Listen, there are waters
Hidden from us
In the maze we find them still
We'll take you to them
You take your young ones
May they take their own in turn
And by our lives be we spirit
And by our hearts be we women
And by our eyes be we open
And by our hands be we whole

FERRON

Additional Readings

Amidei, Nancy. "Women and Powerlessness: A Feminist Analysis." Paper presented at the Women's Symposium; Annual Program Meeting of the Council on Social Work Education, Washington, D.C., February 17, 1985.

Balasson, Mary Lou; Briggs, Thomas L.; and Olson, Miriam M. *Infusing a Male Dominated Medical Setting with Feminist Values: Intervention by a Social Work Team.* Syracuse, N.Y.: Syracuse University School of Social Work, 1981.

Blanton, J. "Women Consulting with Women: Feminist Ideology and Organizational Structure and Process." Paper presented at the Annual Convention of the American Psychological Association, Los Angeles, California, 1981.

Brandwein, Ruth. "Toward the Feminization of Community and Organization Practice." In Armand Lauffer and Edward Newman, eds., *Community Organization in the 80's* (Summer–Fall, 1981), pp. 180–193.

Bricker-Jenkins, Mary, and Joseph, Barbara. "Social Control and Social Change: Toward a Feminist Model of Social Work Practice." Paper presented at the NASW Conference on Social Work Practice in Sexist Society, Washington, D.C., 1980.

Cantarow, Ellen, et al. *Moving the Mountain: Women Working for Social Change.* Old Westbury, N.Y.: Feminist Press, 1980.

Crow, Ginny. "The Process/Product Split," *Quest,* 4 (1978), pp. 15–23.

———; Riddle, Dorothy; and Sparks, Carolyn. "The Process/Product Debate," *Quest,* 4 (1979), pp. 15–36.

Cummerton, Joan. "A Feminine Perspective on Research: What Does It Help Us See?" Paper presented at the Annual Meeting of the Council on Social Work Education, Fort Worth, Texas, March 1983.

Cummings, Joan. "Sexism in Social Work: Some Thoughts on Strategy for Structural Change." Unpublished paper, Maritime School of Social Work, Dalhouse University, Halifax, Nova Scotia, Canada, 1980.

Gluckstern, Norman. "Beyond Therapy: Personal and Institutional Change." In Edna I. Rawlings and Diane K. Carter, eds., *Psychotherapy for Women: Treatment Toward Equality.* Springfield, Ill.: Charles C Thomas, 1977.

Gottlieb, Naomi, ed., *Alternative Social Services for Women.* New York: Columbia University Press, 1980.

Harstock, Nancy. "Feminist Theory and Revolutionary Strategy." In Zillah Eisenstein, ed., *Capitalist Patriarchy and the Call for the Socialist Feminism.* New York: Monthly Review Press, 1979, pp. 71–73.

———. "Political Change: Two Perspectives of Power." *Building Feminist Theory: Essays from Quest.* New York: Longman, 1981, pp. 3–19.

———. "Staying Alive." *Quest,* 3 (1976–77), pp. 2–14.

Hooyman, Nancy. "Redefining Models of Power and Administrative Styles," *Social Development Issues,* 2 (Winter 1978), pp. 46–54.

Johnson, Pauline. "Women and Power: Towards a Theory of Effectiveness," *Journal of Social Issues,* 32 (1976), pp. 99–109.

Joreen. "The Tyranny of Structurelessness." In Anne Koedt et al., eds., *Radical Feminism.* New York: Quadrangle Books, 1973.

Josefowitz, Natasha. *Paths to Power.* Reading, Mass.: Addison-Wesley Publishing Co., 1980.

Kanter, Rosabeth Moss. *Another Voice: Feminist Perspectives on Social Life and Social Service.* Garden City, N.Y.: Doubleday Anchor Books, 1975.

———, and Zurcha, Louis A. "Evaluating Alternatives and Alternative Valuing," *Journal of Applied Behavioral Sciences,* 9 (1973), pp. 381–397.

Lindenfeld, Frank, and Rothschild-Whitt, Joyce. *Workplace Democracy in Social Change.* Boston: Porter Sargent, 1982.

Miller, Jean Baker. *Women and Power.* Wellesley, Mass.: Stone Center for Developmental Services and Studies, 1982.

Morgenbesser, Meg, et al. "The Evolution of Three Alternative Social Service Agencies," *Catalyst,* 11 (1981), pp. 71–83.

Moskol, Marjorie D. "Feminist Theory and Casework Practice." In Bernard Ross and S. K. Khinduka, eds., *Social Work in Practice.* Washington, D.C.: National Association of Social Workers, 1976. Pp. 181–190.

Norman, Elaine, and Mancuso, Arline, eds., *Women's Issues and Social Work Practice.* Itasca, Ill.: F. E. Peacock Publishers, 1980.

Parsons, Patricia, and Hodne, Carol, "A Collective Experiment in Women's Health," *Science for the People* (July–August 1982), pp. 9–13.

Red Apple Collective. "Socialist-Feminist Women's Unions: Past and Present," *Socialist Review,* 8 (March–April 1978).

Riddle, Dorothy. "Integrating Process and Product," *Quest,* 4 (1978), pp. 23–32.

Rothschild-Whitt, Joyce. "The Collective Organization: An Alternative to Rationale-Bureaucratic Models," *American Sociological Review,* 44 (1979), pp. 509–527.

———. "Taking Our Future Seriously," *Quest,* 3 (1976), pp. 17–30.

Weick, Ann. "The Women's Movement as a Paradigm Change," *Social Development Issues,* 2 (Winter 1978), pp. 60–67.

———, and Vandiver, Susan T., eds., *Women, Power, and Change.* Washington, D.C.: National Association of Social Workers, 1982.

Wetzel, Janice Wood. "Interaction of Feminism and Social Work in America." *Social Casework,* 57 (April 1976), pp. 227–236.

Resources

The poetry selections reprinted in this volume and other feminist writings may be obtained at women's bookstores and by mail order. For a list of women's bookstores in the United States, write

Feminist Bookstore News
P.O. Box 882554
San Francisco, California 94188

For annotated bibliographies of feminist and lesbian books available by mail order, write

CHARIS: Books and More
419 Moreland Avenue, N.E.
Atlanta, Georgia 30307

The music may be obtained at many bookstores or by mail order from

Ladyslipper
P.O. Box 3130
Durham, North Carolina 27705

To be added to a nationwide computerized mailing list of persons interested in feminist work, write

National Women's Mailing List
1195 Valenica Street
San Francisco, California 94110

For information on media resources, periodicals, cultural workers, presses, and library collections, write

Index/Directory of Women's Media
Women's Institute for Freedom of the Press
3306 Ross Place, N.W.
Washington, D.C. 20008

For a comprehensive listing of academic and nonacademic feminist publications, write

Annotated Guide to Women's Periodicals in the United States and Canada
The Women's Programs Office
Earlham College
Richmond, Indiana 47374

For a guide to the social science literature on women and women's issues, write

Work on Women: A Guide to the Literature
Mary Evans and David Morgan, eds.
Tavistock Publications
c/o Methuen & Co.
733 Third Avenue
New York, N.Y. 10017

For a subscription to a monthly publication on the new and recent feminist literature, write

Women's Review of Books
Wellesley College Center for Research on Women
Wellesley, Massachusetts 02181

For news and analyses from a reformist feminist perspective, write

National Organization for Women
425 13th Street, N.W.
Washington, D.C. 20004

For a subscription to a monthly periodical on news and analyses of the movement from a radical feminist perspective, write

Off Our Backs
1841 Columbia Road, N.W.
Washington, D.C. 20009

For news and analyses from a socialist feminist perspective, write

Women Organizing
1300 West Belmont
Chicago, Illinois 60657

CATALYST: A Socialist Journal of the Social Services
Box 1144, Cathedral Station
New York, New York 10025

For a bibliography on women of color, see

Selected Bibliography on Social Science Readings on Women of Color, from
Center for Research on Women
Memphis State University
Memphis, Tennessee 38152

For a new periodical by and for women of color, write

Between Ourselves
P.O. Box 1939
Washington, D.C. 20013

126   *Not for Women Only*

For information on women of color in the United States and internationally, write

Third World Women's Archives Newsletter
P.O. Box 2651
Peter Stuyvesant Station
New York, New York 10009

For lesbian feminist news and analyses (available free to lesbians although dona-
tions are appreciated), write

Lesbian Connection
Helen Diner Memorial Women's Center/Ambitious Amazons
P.O. Box 881
East Lansing, Michigan 48823

For a lesbian-feminist research newsletter, write

Matrices
Jacquelyn N. Zita, Managing Editor
Women's Studies
Ford Hall 492
University of Minnesota
Minneapolis, Minnesota 55455

For a quarterly publication from the feminist men's movement, write

Brothers
David Mattison, Chair
Communications Committee
National Organization for Changing Men
814 Blackhawk Drive
University Park, Illinois 60466

For an international networking publication covering women's spirituality and
traditional healing work, write

Of a Like Mind
P.O. Box 6021
Madison, Wisconsin 53716

For a quarterly publication that explores the links between women's spirituality
and politics, write

Woman of Power
P.O. Box 827
Cambridge, Massachusetts 02238